One hundred years ago, a Russian physician named Nicholas Russel (alias Nikolai Konstantinovich Sudzilovskii) stormed the Golden State from San Francisco to Soapweed and penned an unvarnished account of campers and cranks, country dances and cutthroat capitalism.

Russel's testy travelogue—entertaining, outspoken, often outraged, sometimes outrageous—was unearthed a century later in a Moscow archive by Stanford historian Terence Emmons, who oversaw its translation. Emmons's further inquiry into Russel's bizarre background yields the portrait of a man whose cantankerous spirit eventually led him into a dogfight with the Russian Orthodox Church, election to the presidency of the Hawaiian Senate, paternity at age 68, and a plan to incite an invasion of pre-Revolutionary Russia by Mongolian partisans.

The result? *Around California in 1891*—a feisty slice of California history the Chamber of Commerce may have forgotten to mention.

Around California in 1891

TERENCE EMMONS

**The
Portable Stanford
Book Series**

Published by the
Stanford Alumni Association

THE PORTABLE STANFORD is a book series sponsored by the Stanford Alumni Association. The series is designed to bring the widest possible sampling of Stanford's intellectual resources into the homes of alumni. It includes books based on current research as well as books that deal with philosophical issues, which by their nature reflect to a greater degree the personal views of their authors.

THE PORTABLE STANFORD BOOK SERIES
Stanford Alumni Association
Bowman Alumni House
Stanford, California 94305-4005

Library of Congress Catalog Card
Number: 91-065718
ISBN: 0-916318-46-X

Printed in the United States of America

10 9 8 7 6 5 4 3 2 1

Acknowledgments

This project owes much to Jehanne Gheith, who transcribed Russel's handwritten manuscript; to Sara Fenander, who translated Russel's Russian into English; and to Bert Patenaude, who provided crucial materials from The National Archives. Editor Bruce Goldman and Production Manager Amy Pilkington of the Portable Stanford Book Series went beyond the call of professional duty in the care and dispatch they bestowed, respectively, on the manuscript and the illustrations that accompany the text.

Further thanks go to the Department of History, Stanford University, which defrayed some of this project's expenses in recognition of the University's Centennial year, 1991.

Series Editor and Manager: Bruce Goldman
Production Manager: Amy Pilkington
Cover Designer: Paul Carstensen

Table of Contents

Preface

Nicholas John Russel was a Russian émigré whose vivid account of his travels throughout the California of a century ago were discovered recently by Terence Emmons in a Moscow archive. For all his unique biography, Russel stands squarely in a venerable tradition of ambivalent commentary about the Golden State.

"Never be betrayed into disparaging California," Stanford University's first president, David Starr Jordan, inscribed in his notebook in 1891. Yet before a decade was out, Jordan was writing that "California is commercially asleep, that her industries

are gambling ventures, that her local politics is in the hands of professional pickpockets, that her small towns are the shabbiest in Christendom, that her saloons control more constituents than her churches, that she is the slave of corporations, that she knows no such thing as public opinion, that she has not yet learned to distinguish enterprise from highway robbery, nor reform from blackmail."

That Jordan broke his self-imposed protocol, and did so with such vehemence, typified the effect that California had on late-19th-century observers. In the idea of California they often invested their most extravagant hopes; in the reality of California those hopes were inevitably tempered, and sometimes cruelly broken.

Russel recorded many of the same features of California life that attracted Jordan's attention—the state's apparent corruption, the complexity and rudeness of its politics, the astonishing variety of its peoples, the grandeur of its scenery, and the precious, fragile hopes that breathed upon this last golden land. While all of his observations and judgments are suffused by the peculiar coloration of his own rather remarkable background, described in detail later in this book by Professor Emmons, Russel's century-old account serves to remind us that "California Dreamin'" is an enterprise with a long and varied pedigree—and no doubt a considerable future.

David M. Kennedy
William Robertson Coe Professor of History and American Studies
Chairman, Department of History
Stanford University

Preface

Introduction

California in the late 1880s and early 1890s was in a state of flux unusual even for California. It was a time of rapid population growth and land boom, spurred on by advertising campaigns; of labor unrest and uproar over Chinese immigration; of growing public outrage over the railroad and land monopolies and the closely related issue of corruption in local politics. In 1880, at the end of 22 years spent in California, Henry George had published his *Progress and Poverty*, with its theory of a single tax and fulminations against absentee land speculators. The progressives and the muckrakers were waiting in the wings to do battle against the railroad monopoly and political corruption.

San Francisco was still the center of the state's political and economic life, and nearly a third of the California population lived in what we know today as the Bay Area. In October 1887, the same year that William Randolph Hearst took over the *San Francisco Examiner* and the Pacific Railway Commission undertook its investigation of the business practices of "The Big Four"—Leland Stanford, Mark Hopkins, Collis P. Huntington, and Charles Crocker—there rode into town on the Big Four's railroad one Nicholas John Russel, MD.

This unremarkable Anglo-Saxon–appearing name was borne by a remarkable and decidedly non–Anglo-Saxon individual. Its owner was a Russian revolutionary who had fled abroad to avoid arrest in his native country, had then gotten his medical degree from the University of Bucharest in Romania, and had spent a number of years practicing medicine and dabbling in revolutionary politics and journalism in Switzerland, France, England, and the Balkans before immigrating to the United States. He was 37 when he arrived in San Francisco.

Russel was a man of many parts, and one of them was literary. Almost everywhere he went after leaving Western Europe for more-exotic regions, he wrote accounts of the places he visited for Russian highbrow magazines, using pseudonyms. He did this writing partly for pleasure, no doubt, but also with the prospect of gain. These accounts typically combined observations about local flora, fauna, and topography with socioeconomic and political commentary.

Russel's description of California, "Around California" (*Po Kalifornii*), presented here in English translation, was one of the first such efforts Russel made. Unlike most of the others, it was never published. Indeed, Russel carried the manuscript all the way to China. From there, in 1926, it made its way along with the rest of his papers to the Russian Historical Archive Abroad in Prague, Czechoslovakia. In 1945 the Prague Archive was taken to Moscow, and Russel's papers were eventually lodged in the Archive of the October Revolution. There, while researching materials on 19th-century Russian radicals in America, I found Russel's handwritten manuscript.

Apparently Russel had not finished his "Around California," which he clearly intended for a Russian readership, when he pulled up stakes and moved on to Hawaii. There he began to write about the even more exotic landscapes and humankind of the islands and forgot about his California project. The manuscript cannot be dated exactly, but internal evidence and the time of Russel's departure indicate that the writing was done between late 1891 and early 1892, while his last summer of travel in search of material for the account must have been the summer of 1891. The manuscript breaks off after a few lines of a new, eleventh, chapter (omitted here), in which Russel intended to describe a trip from the gold country to Lake Tahoe.

While many of the social and political issues touched on in Russel's account will be familiar to readers of California history, "Around California" brings a fresh and unusual perspective to life in the area exactly a century ago—that of a Russian radical writing for a Russian audience.

Russel brought with him to California many preconceptions, and not all of them stemmed from his radicalism. Take, for example, his attitude toward Jews, as revealed in his remarks about Galician salesmen and "Messrs. Weinstock and Lubin" of Sacramento. In this case, the source is not, of course, revolutionary ideology but Russel's roots in West Russia. Russel's home territory lay within the Pale of Jewish Settlement, mostly the provinces taken from Poland in the partitions, which had brought the Russian Empire most of its Jewish population. Jews were generally restricted to this territory and could not own land.

Consequently, Jews constituted an urban element predominantly engaged in commerce; in many towns of the Pale the population was overwhelmingly Jewish. In these conditions, stereotypes of Jewish sharp dealing and parasitism flourished among the Christian population, both peasant and gentry. In this, and no doubt in other ways, too, Russel was more tied to tradition than he would have liked to admit.

But Russel's critical perspectives on California should not be attributed entirely to his preconceptions: On many subjects, such as the railroadmen's business practices, monopolistic tendencies, Chinese labor, and so on, Russel's remarks simply reflected what he could read every day in the San Francisco newspapers. For example: The "Big Four" railroad magnates and their excess profits, monopolistic dominance of western commerce, and alleged buying of political influence were the perennial targets of the San Francisco newspapers. (Although their names still liberally adorn the geography of the city and its environs, Stanford and his partners generally had a bad press in San Francisco throughout the late 19th century). Moreover, in 1887, the year Russel arrived in town, a major congressional investigation into the Big Four's business practices was underway. The congressional commission's condemnation of their practices made Russel's pale by comparison.[1] Even his remark that Stanford built his university "in an attempt to pacify public opinion" was undoubtedly something Russel picked up from the local newspapers.[2]

While in San Francisco, Nicholas Russel, typically, did not restrict his activities to practicing medicine and writing. He also got involved in a scandal-ridden campaign to discredit the Russian Orthodox Bishop of The Aleutians and Alaska, whose diocesan residence was in San Francisco. Some aspects of the story made the headlines at the time, but others were avoided by the press, and it was soon forgotten. This is an interesting story in its own right, but also for what it reveals about Russel, the Russian Church and State, and the San Francisco scene.

The second part of this book tells that story, drawing on contemporary press accounts and on the records of the Russian Consulate General in San Francisco. It does so against the background of an account of Russel's life before he reached California. The story of "The Bishop and the Schoolboys" is followed by a brief description of Russel's adventures after he left California and, finally, some comments about Russel's views on American civilization from the perspective of his ideology in general and his "Around California" in particular.

Thus, as both author and historical actor, Russel takes us "Around California in 1891."

Terence Emmons
Department of History
Stanford University
May 24, 1991

Part I

TIME TABLE.
Sacramento and Placerville Railroad.

Stations.	Leave. Pas.	Leave. Ft.	Arrive. Pas.	Arrive. Ft.
	A.M.	A.M.	P.M.	A.M.
Placerville	11..35	6..00	7..25	11..10
Diamond Spgs..	11..47	6..18	7..09	10..55
El Dorado... ..	11.53	6..28	6..59	10..48
Cummings......	....	....	...	..
Shingle Springs	12..11	6..55	6..32	10..28
Bennett	....	....	.	....
Dugan.........	....	....	....	....
Brandon........	....	....	....	....
Bryant.........	....	....	....	....
Latrobe	....	....	....	...
Cothrin	....	...	....	....
White Rock....	....	....	....	....
Sacramento.....	2..40	11..35	3 10	6..35
	Arrive		Leave.	

Trains do not run on Sunday.

1

Roughing It

Surely, one of the unique features of American life worthy of imitation is the widespread practice of spending summer vacation in the wilderness camping or wandering. Migratory instinct and love of nature are deeply ingrained in the human heart, and many centuries of settled city life will no doubt be required to extinguish them. Until then, "camping," "tramping," and "roughing it," as Americans call this custom of summer traveling, will not lose their poetic charm and will continue to be the inexpensive and popular source of a multitude of healthy and varied pleasures.

The relative scarcity of population, and the abundance of as yet unoccupied or unexploited places, favor this pastime. In western Europe, where one runs into some sort of "Forbidden" notice at every step—signs prohibiting walking on the grass, picking fruit, or even simply walking on paths, placed across each sacred piece of private property—this sort of custom would be unthinkable. Another favorable condition in America is the complete absence of such obstacles to traveling as an internal passport system.

The rural inhabitants are so accustomed to the city dwellers' seasonal travels that they not only do not obstruct them, but rather encourage them in all the ways they can. And they have not a few of their own practical reasons for this. As is known, unlike farmers in Europe the agrarian population of the States lives not in villages and settlements but on separate, scattered, single farms. For the isolated farmer, the simple appearance of a human being is pleasant in and of itself. Solitude can bore just about anyone, not excluding the American. With the crowd that appears, you can talk about political and other news and also boast about your successes on the farm. You can probably sell them some of the family produce: bread, eggs, butter, vegetables. The most important point, however, is that the more visitors there are, the more the public gets to know the area, the sooner people will take over and buy up land, the faster the area is settled—and the price of land grows proportionately. By the way, the farmers aren't overly willing to point out free or state property, and they do it only if they take a liking to somebody and hope that he will become a good neighbor, or, ultimately, just for a certain sum of money. They prefer to conceal these free plots from chance passers-by (among whom are many seekers of free land), thinking instead of relatives or friends. But they never have any objection to selling their own plot for a profit.

People camp and travel all over America for all sorts of

reasons. Sometimes people resort to very original schemes. I know of an instance when, to satisfy their wanderlust, two poor young girls turned up on a railway line that was being built and opened a canteen for the workers in a tent. They moved along with their tent at the same rate as the work and, in this manner, not only did they lead a gypsy life all summer, they also made some money.

However, nowhere else has camping life become so rooted as on the western side of the Rocky Mountains, and especially in California. Here, one more thing must be added to the list of

Courtesy, The Bancroft Library

An isolated California farmhouse, 1891

reasons above: the sharp division of the year into the rainy winter and dry summer seasons. Leaving for their trips from May to November, the travelers don't have to worry about rain, which makes the travel much simpler and easier.

In all probability, it was the pioneers seeking new lands, cattle herders, gold prospectors, and other migrants by necessity who laid the groundwork for summer travels. And there are still many of that sort of people in the West even now. People usually go on their trips in families or small groups of close friends and acquaintances. A man or woman teacher, priest, lawyer, high school or college student, clerk of either gender, small renter, shopkeeper—anyone who can take a couple of weeks or months away from business for summer vacation—doesn't hesitate to find him- or herself a companion or companions for a camping trip.

For those who don't have enough time to undertake a long camping trip on their own, enterprising people have built camps in the environs of San Francisco on the ocean, on the Russian River (which got its name from a former Russian settlement), and in other exceptionally picturesque spots with good climates. Here, for $1.00–2.50 a day, you can rent a prepared tent with bedding, service, and meals. All the chores are done for you; your time is completely at your disposal. The camp owners are generally very tolerant people, not much like our hotel owners. They are glad to be of help to you, try not to constrain you in any way, and for all these extras are satisfied with the most reasonable payment. They take guests under all manner of arrangements; for instance, they rent just the tent and let you take care of food, or even set up your own tent for a small compensation as rent for the land.

No matter how attractive and popular summer camping is, far from everybody does it. First of all, it should be noted that Americans as a lot suffer from an obsession with profit to the detriment of all other human needs. To be rich—and, being rich, to be even richer, to double and triple already colossal fortunes—constitutes something like an innate need. The American dreams about this sleeping and waking, all his thoughts are directed toward this; he looks at everything else only as a means. Insatiable passion for profit drives him to the point where he doesn't have time or sense to eat, rest, or enjoy himself. He eats breakfast and lunch, as it were, on the run, swallowing hurriedly, hardly chewing whatever is available, with scant concern about the taste and quality of what has been swallowed. His entertainments—the theater, concerts, the club, outings, parties, balls, ball games, horse races, and boxing matches—are simply a part of business. He goes to these events not so much to relax or enjoy himself, but because he anticipates meeting the right man, making the right acquaintance, saying the right thing; to make a significant impression, or win a bet, or whatever. From the day of his birth to the moment of his death he never has time; there is never any time. His nerves are strained to the limit and his thoughts always revolve around the same object. Profit, getting rich, first are regarded as a key to the gates of heaven, and then rapidly become identical to heaven itself. Maybe he is right after all—at least for America, where everything is bought and sold, where all doors are opened with the key of gold, where popular opinion values people according to the weight of the dollars they possess.

This feature of the American character does not allow most Americans to take advantage of summer leisure. To tear oneself away from business, even for a few days, is not just a sacrifice, but a crime for which an American's conscience will reproach him many long years. That's why significant numbers of so-called "respectable and upright businessmen" decide to take a vacation for two or three days, many for a week or two, only if their families or doctors absolutely demand it. Ironically, from the standpoint of simple common sense, this type of person requires more rest than anybody else. Among them it is difficult to find a man who doesn't suffer from nervous exhaustion, which has become the American national disease. The notorious American "dyspepsia," without which it is difficult to imagine an American, is in most cases only the partial expression of a general exhaustion of the nervous system.

Of course in our mercantile century, profit occupies no small part of the human soul in the rest of the civilized world; but this passion has not yet reached uniform proportions. In the rest of the world this motivation for human actions is not yet openly recognized, is not equated with virtue, and, thus, is covered with a veil as are certain other natural needs. In America, alas, the veil is no longer required. Public opinion values and respects the acquisitive talent. It is included as a vital element in prevailing ideals of respectability and human perfection. You can be proud of it.

If this sort of life-style continues for another century and, in addition, the constant immigration from Europe stops, it's difficult to say what fate awaits the American people. The young generation already clearly shows consequent symptoms of overexhaustion, lack of vitality, and degeneration. Morphine addicts, cocaine addicts, alcoholics, opium smokers are all around. It's awful to behold this young generation.

The American buys his material well-being for a dear price, and you can envy him in this only from a distance. This is why you rarely encounter a businessman among campers when you go on a camping trip. You won't meet a rich aristocrat there, either. I say rich aristocrat because, in America, to be rich and to be an aristocrat is one and the same. Rich people—and, following their example, the members of the middle class who try to keep up with them—don't spend their short vacations with the simple goals of entertainment or relaxation, but rather strive to show themselves off. A whole line of fashionable luxury hotels, one more expensive than the next, has been built for them, barracks-like, along the southern coast of the Great Ocean from San Francisco to San Diego. To spend a week or two under the same roof as multimillionaire Stanford or Hopkins is considered not only enviable, but a necessary signal indicating that one belongs to the "best society." Many bourgeois families without the means for such a summer pilgrimage to mammon's shrine lock themselves away behind closed shutters, give their servants a holiday and spend days and weeks in solitary confinement living on locusts and wild honey [Matthew 3:4] so that when the time runs out, they can show off to their neighbors, announcing that they had returned from Monterey or Coronado Beach, where they had a glorious time!

The reader can imagine these rich aristocrats by recalling the heroes of *The Luck of Roaring Camp* by Bret Harte: gold

Courtesy, The Bancroft Library

The Palace Hotel, San Francisco, ca. 1890

prospectors, tavern and shop keepers, now of course transformed into upright bourgeois: washed, shaven, well dressed, adorned with heavy watch chains, half-pound gold rings with big diamonds, and with rounded bellies. The bestial expression produced by the strong, underthrust jaw and face overgrown with hair has been complicated by a haughtily self-satisfied, majestic look of Jupiter, developed in part under the influence of general kowtowing, and also because of the money-maker's own realization that he has accomplished everything terrestrial.

This is the portrait of the real-life equivalent of "Dick,"* now a senator in California, patron and benefactor of his people, who holds shares of coal, railroads, gold, oil, concrete, banks, and other grandiose enterprises, together with which he also holds political power in the great republic. This is the terrible American Jupiter, who emerged from manure, passed through trials and tribulations, and tore himself out of the noose to, at last, win himself a position which many sovereign princes would rightly envy.

Such are the distinguished guests in these fashionable hotels. On the other hand, the service personnel for the most part are the starving intelligentsia: students whose goal is to earn some money during the summer so they can get through the next academic year, writers whose articles haven't sold, inventors who haven't got the money to take out patents for their inventions, lawyers who haven't found clients because they can't establish a respectably appointed office. Not only is the help prohibited from speaking to the guests, but they cannot even sit down in their presence; you can spend a whole month in one of these hotels without hearing a single word from these hotel workers besides the short official "Yes, sir," and "No, sir." If this

* "Dick" is a character from Bret Harte's *The Luck of Roaring Camp*. Russel may have had Leland Stanford in mind here.

prohibition did not exist, the lackey would be able to stump his lord time and again.

In Europe fashionable "watering places" (due to official tension, formality, all that's known as etiquette and good manners) do not have the reputation of being pleasant retreats. But here, the exaggeration and demanding nature of the dressed-up Dick and fawning would-be courtiers know no bounds and completely poison existence.

Chained year-round to his factory machine, the city worker also rarely travels in the summer. He has essentially no leisure time and takes pleasure in short Sunday trips out of town, picnics, and the like, which are also very fashionable in California, probably for the same reasons as camping. Every Sunday morning (other holidays in America are very rare) special trains and steamboats shuttle tens of thousands of city dwellers around the area. For the most part these are trade unions, fraternal societies, and other workers' organizations, who go on picnics. Usually an out-of-town park is selected for this event, where they organize races, ball games, and dances with all possible prizes and awards, and then lunch in a pavilion or outside, an affair during which a huge number of sandwiches and cookies are consumed. Toward evening—after they have made a lot of noise, run all over the place and eaten their fill—the crowds return to the city, in order to appear again at the factory machine at six o'clock on Monday morning.

So, strictly speaking, the middle class, which is quite large in America, goes camping: that is, the petite bourgeoisie and intelligentsia, which, in the States, are much closer to one another and much farther from the "aristocrat" than anywhere else.

Camping parties are usually planned and organized in winter or spring. Willing participants are recruited; the itinerary is plotted; expenses are estimated; tents are prepared. When everything is ready, either the party proceeds by train to a certain point where they hire one or two carts, or they find horses

Courtesy, The Bancroft Library

A camping group lunches in the forest, Yosemite, ca. 1890

locally and the travelers immediately set off on horses. Essential items for a trip are a field kitchen, enough provisions (especially canned goods), fishing and hunting gear, camera, axe, saw, etc.

When you reach the desired area, an appropriate spot is chosen in the forest or on the bank of a stream. The carts are unloaded; the tents are pitched; a temporary camp is set up. The burden of necessary jobs is divided as democratically as possible among the participants. One cooks, another prepares the firewood, another fishes or hunts for game for the kitchen. In free time each does what he pleases. Botanists examine the flora; artists paint from nature; writers draw inspiration from the local scenery and compose their verses or write articles. After staying for several days and trampling the interesting surroundings to their heart's content, the camp moves on.

11

Roughing It

2

San Francisco and Environs

It was the end of May. Despite the early hour, San Francisco was already on its feet. The cable cars, stuffed with workers hurrying to the factory, ran like chains back and forth along its streets. Carters, with their enormous carts drawn by several pairs of mighty horses, bobbed noisily among them, as did provenders in their light wagons, delivering milk, vegetables, dry goods, and other groceries. In terms of the amount of noise and traffic at this time of day, this city is the equal of New York, London, and other large port cities.

We arrived at the dock and bought our tickets. The ferryboat was to take us across the bay to the neighboring town of Oakland, where the railroad station is located. This crossing takes half an hour and is one of the most pleasant out-of-town excursions. Wherever you look, the landscape is magnificent, reminiscent of southern Italy. The enormous bay, which could easily contain all the world's fleets, is dotted with small, hilly, picturesque islands; unfortunately, they remain bare, as the government has retained them with the intent of turning them into fortifications should the need arise. In individualistic America, more than in any other country, the saying "Everybody's interest is nobody's interest" applies to government and municipal institutions as a whole. If these islands belonged to private individuals, they would have been covered long since with gardens and pretty country houses like the ones that peek coquettishly from the other side of the bay.

The view is best from the middle of the bay. From here, looking back westward beyond the port's forest of masts and steamboat stacks, San Francisco can be clearly seen spreading out in straight lines on the hillsides. In the lower, industrial part of the city, black smoke pours forth, its regular columns rising high into the sky from the numerous factories and mills. The buildings in this quarter are notable solely for their dimensions and barracks-like vulgarity. But further away and higher up, the city is both attractive and original. Except for several dozen large stone mansions, which unsuccessfully imitate the styles of all epochs and nations, belong to the lords of commerce, and are concentrated in two or three fashionable blocks, the rest of the city consists of adorable, comfortable wooden cottages, painted in bright colors, English-style. Most of them are two- or three-storied, with the obligatory bay window. Were it not for their tendency to the vertical, and (due to lack of space) their crowding, and if there were more gardens and greenery around, I would compare them with our dachas, the kind you can see when approaching Moscow or Petersburg.

Courtesy, The Bancroft Library

Market Street from Third Street, San Francisco, looking east

To the east, at the foot of the high hills on the opposite side of the bay, the small towns of Alameda and Oakland sprawl a bit more spaciously in verdant gardens and parks. Essentially, they are just suburbs of San Francisco. The majority of their inhabitants spend only the night at home, while except for holidays they spend all day in the metropolis, arriving in the morning and returning home in the evening. Because of the very low fare ($3 a month), this is even more convenient and, in any case, more healthy than living in the city proper.

The end of the bay is not visible to the south. There, in a pale bluish haze, the water's blue imperceptibly becomes the blue of the sky. To the north, in addition to the already mentioned islands, you can see the fairly high, partially forested mountains of the coastal range, and a new group of towns that are even more picturesque because of their higher elevation and abundance of vegetation: Sausalito, San Rafael, and others.

The morning was peaceful and sunny. Because of the distance, the surrounding landscape was shrouded in transparent light-blue fog. The sun had just risen, and its rays had not yet dispersed the invigorating morning freshness; they played merrily in a light ripple on the ocean's blue surface and sparkled like multicolored lights in the spray of the paddle wheels. The sun illuminating the coquettish little towns, the mountainous heights rising above them, and the islands, half-rocky and half-adorned with fresh vegetation, is a visual effect difficult to convey in words. Only those who know the panoramas of Swiss lakes, Naples, and Sicily could imagine this scene.

Yes, nature here is miraculously beautiful. When you look at it, your mood becomes optimistic and idealistic, only to be stifled when you think of the sharp contrast between nature and the petty-mercenary vulgar-materialistic spirit of this human anthill. The spiritual impoverishment of life escapes the usual tourist's notice. Nothing prevents him from being carried away by nature and projecting its beauty onto the local inhabitants. He is unwittingly won over by the visible display of prosperity, wealth, and even splendor abetted by preconceived notions from reading about the republic's freedom and equality; it's not surprising that the portrait of America painted in our country's press, and particularly the image of California, is something like an earthly paradise. The fact that our tourists arrive to sightsee with stuffed pockets and good philistine digestion contributes to their optimism in no small way. If it weren't for that—if they were to come here like the thousands of immigrants who arrive every day from Europe and the eastern part of America (that is, in special trains for immigrants) and were doomed to an arduous and long struggle to make a living in the midst of this paradise—the picture they would paint of American well-being would darken considerably.

This time, however, we do not intend to take the reader behind the scenes of American life. On the contrary, I will take him to the place where there is more light and less shadow, into the forests and the mountains—into the charming heart of the Golden State where gold was first discovered, to the places described by Bret Harte, the so-called El Dorado County, of which Placerville is the administrative center.

The ferries that depart for the other side of the bay every quarter of an hour are luxuriously furnished. Several of them have electric lighting, and in the evening they seem like floating fairytale palaces. The lower deck is reserved for freight, carriages, and smokers. Also located here are the bar, the restaurant, and

Courtesy, The Bancroft Library

San Francisco Bay seen from Telegraph Hill, ca. 1891

a tall chair for a Negro who shines shoes. Although there are no required sections for different classes, and although everybody pays the same fare for the crossing and has the same rights, the public nevertheless voluntarily divides itself into two classes. All those who are poorer and dirtier prefer the lower, dirty deck; all those who are cleaner rise to the top in the huge, splendid hall, its floor covered in velvet and its walls hung with mirrors and oil paintings, which quite respectably depict the scenery of the Golden State.

Because the continental shore of the bay is shallow, the dock and the train station are built on a small artificial island, some distance from the shore, to which they are connected by a long viaduct. The station, like the ferry, is divided into the same two levels, which, at docking, are connected by separate gangplanks to the two corresponding levels of the ferry. Not only does this expedite the vessel's unloading process, but it also gives both classes the opportunity to avoid mixing.

The Alameda Ferry

Oakland, Alameda, & Berkeley Ferry Building, San Francisco

The upper level of the station is an enormous, luxurious, excellently lit hall, kept in a state of cleanliness befitting a permanent exhibition of all manner of merchandise and announcements. The lower hall is dark and dirty. As you leave the station, several trains stand waiting to depart for various destinations indicated by large signs. Everybody can easily locate his train. Bells are not customary here. You arrive, board the train, and continue on.

The lack of policemen and the absence of people dressed in special uniforms is also surprising for the European. Neither on the ferry, nor in the station, nor on the street do you encounter anyone in military or other uniform. Nonetheless, a surprising orderliness somehow prevails of its own accord. This enormous crowd of different types, numbering several thousand, debarks peacefully without noise or collisions, and people seat themselves in the train cars wherever and however they please. Some stand on the platforms, others prefer the smoking car and even the baggage section. However, most everybody—and, of course, all the women—sit in the usual passenger cars, which are general seating and similar to our second-class cars, but longer and more spacious. Oddly, in most cases there are two or three times more cars than would be necessary if all the seats were filled. In this respect the American railway companies are very liberal. Not only do they not pack the cars full of people like sardines, they even allow passengers absolute freedom to move around. True, in exceptional cases, there are twice as many passengers as there are seats, but then the passengers are tolerant of the company and don't demand seats only because they've been sold tickets and stand in the aisles holding onto the straps.

What positively poisons the existence of the foreigner unaccustomed to America is the advertising. It goes without saying that in population centers it exists in all imaginable possible and impossible forms; but on the road as well, whether on the railroad, ferry boat, or country lane, it flies into your ears and nose like mosquitoes in the swamps or woods. It spoils the landscape every step of the way and constantly reminds you of buying and selling. In this respect, Americans' inventiveness knows no bounds. The docks and stations are literally plastered with gigantic, garish announcements and pictures specially designed to attract attention. Along railroad viaducts and rights-of-way, on trees, sometimes near the summits of distant hills, we are informed for the umpteenth time that such-and-such a newspaper has the largest number of subscribers, so-and-so's pills have miraculous curative powers for all diseases, and such-and-such a soap is superior to all the other soaps in the world. With all due allowance for the mercantile spirit of the age, you must agree that anybody would find this irritating.

But the traveler's torments do not end here. No sooner have you taken your seat and the train has begun to move than a gentleman with a basket appears in the car and unceremoniously throws two or three nuts at each passenger, paying no attention to whether they hit you in the eye or mouth. The passengers take this in stride, and most, for lack of anything better to do, crack the nuts and eat them. The gentleman disappears without asking for payment, but five minutes later he reappears to see whose appetite has been whetted—and, this time, to sell several dozen bags. After him appears a similar beneficent gentleman with books and newspapers, who, without asking, heaps them upon you and everybody else in hopes of getting you interested; and once you're engrossed in the reading, he will come up as you're on the most interesting page and ask to be paid. Then come the chestnuts, candies, cigars, followed in turn by a procession of new benefactors extremely concerned with such questions as how your baggage will be delivered from the station to the hotel, which hotel would be the most comfortable and cheapest for you to stay in, which restaurant would be appropriate for lunch and dinner, and so on, and so on without end. All these persons have paid the railway company no small sum for the right to poison the passengers' existence, and this tribute is levied a hundredfold from their victims. It is rather dangerous to have dealings with them.

But here is the station. Here, the licensed hawkers are joined by a whole horde of unlicensed ones. Hundreds of all sorts of leaflets and announcements pour onto you through the windows and doors. Some poor chap insisted that I stay in his recommended "very best" hotel. When, to get away from him, I answered that I would stay in my own house, with a genuine but bitter smile he called me a lucky man, one to be envied; if he had his own house, he wouldn't have to bother every traveler passing through, just like a persistent fly, so he could earn a couple of pennies from the hotel owner.

Upon leaving the station you encounter a huge commotion. Imagine twenty or thirty—and in a large city, a hundred—young men chosen for their loud voices. Each one of them represents a hotel. Each holds a packet of address cards, on his cap he wears the name of his hotel in bronze letters. As soon as the doors open and the public surges toward the exit, there is a hellish din that could give a nervous person an attack. Like a flock of vultures, this mob throws itself on its victims and literally tears apart the indecisive people, fighting over them among each other.

In this respect, of the many countries where I have been able to travel, the United States reminds me most of Galicia, where it seems a man is not free from buying and selling even in the grave; there, I once had to brandish a revolver to defend my right to respite from the Jewish salesmen.

I trust the reader will forgive me all these digressions. It's difficult to avoid them when talking about a distant, different country, too little known to us—about our antipodes, whose existence is based on foundations diametrically opposed to ours.

23

San Francisco and Environs

3

On Railroads and the Road to Sacramento

The route to Sacramento, the administrative capital of the state, lies along the eastern side of the enormous bay and in one spot even crosses one of its numerous inlets. Here, the train is loaded onto a ferry and crosses the inlet in this manner. The surroundings are of little interest. The railroad stretches out in a thin band across the wide valley, on both sides of which mountain ranges can be seen through the bluish haze.

The train rolls over salt marshes and low places covered with the so-called California oak, which here they call the black oak. Its overall appearance and the shape of its leaves do not at all resemble our oak. It is a very awkward tree, and rather ugly, because of its misshapen growth, bumpiness, and dryness; in its general shape and leaf type, it resembles the willow, but it is harder and thus makes better firewood, although it is not useful for anything else. In many places, wide expanses are covered with the California poppy (*Eschscholtzia*), a small herbaceous plant with very beautiful yellow-orange flowers, the shape of which resembles our ordinary poppy, grown in gardens in Europe. This is its native country; and it unabashedly takes advantage of its rights as citizen of the Golden State, filling whole meadows, giving them an extraordinary blinding golden color.

Sometimes the railway veers away from the bay and runs for a long while along endless gorges filled with enormous straight rows of vineyards, peach, and other fruit plantations. Since most of the gold has been mined, orchards and wineries are currently the most important elements of production in California. Both are conducted on a large scale with large amounts of capital and with the widest possible use of steam and mechanization. Only under these conditions is there enough profit to pay the scandalous transport fees levied by the railroad monopolists for delivery to the eastern states. A significant amount of fruit doesn't leave California in its fresh form, but rather is canned or preserved. A portion of the grape crop is made into wine and cognac. All these branches of industry, like most production in the States, are already monopolized by a few rich companies, while small farms and orchards, which decrease in number each year, play a rather pathetic role. In San Francisco there are two or three large fruit canneries, and the fate of the small orchardman depends upon the prices they fix. Essentially, he is nothing more than a free-lancer for the land, bank, industrial, and railway companies.

Three lines now connect the Atlantic Ocean with the Pacific: the Northern, the Central, and the Southern. A fourth line—the

Courtesy, The Bancroft Library

Southern Pacific Passenger Depot, San Francisco, ca. 1875

Canadian—crosses the continent outside the United States in Anglo-Canadian territory. Besides these four lines, there is a direct steamboat connection across the Isthmus of Panama with a transfer via the Panamanian railway, as well as a sailing vessel route around South America. The Central and Northern railroads were built by a private company with money from the federal government on the condition that the capital and interest would be repaid during a certain period. In addition, the company was rewarded with huge plots of government land on either side along the whole line (about 25 miles). Neither the capital nor the interest has been repaid, on the grounds of unprofitability; the company was in fact poor and barely made ends meet, but that did not prevent the directors and shareholders from reaping millions. With these millions—as if it were already his own money—Stanford, the head of the enterprise (the same Stanford who, in an attempt to pacify public opinion, recently built a university near San Francisco), together with several cohorts built the so-called Southern Pacific, a new competing line. This is how things stand now: In return for their defaulting on the loan of $70 million, the government is supposed to confiscate the Central Pacific line that was built with its money. But Stanford and Co. don't give a damn. "Confiscate it," they say. "Now we have our own line."

But pending confiscation, all three lines—the Northern, the Central, and the Southern—are for all intents and purposes in the hands of one company. This company pays significant sums each year to the Canadian-English railroad and the two steamship companies, on the condition that they will not take freight to California at rates lower than the company tariff. Thus the whole state—or, it's better to say, the whole Pacific coast, namely, Washington, Oregon, and California—depend completely on one company for their connections with the eastern part of America; and this company, of course, unabashedly takes advantage of this by taxing merchandise and passengers to the maximum they can bear. Some trading firms prefer, and even find it profitable, to send their merchandise between California and New York via England as a way to free themselves slightly from this iron grip.

Incidentally, along the route to Sacramento is one of the largest representatives of California wineries, the so-called Inglenook (corner near a hearth), extravagantly furnished as the country residence of an American millionaire, valued at a million dollars and belonging to Mr. Gustav Niebaum, the Finnish-born vice-president of the former Alaska Fur Seal Company who recently served as the Russian Consul.

As you pass by these endless orchards and vineyards, it is amazing how comparatively few populated areas there are. Except for Benicia, a small village located on the bay shore centered around a naval ship dock, there are only one or two settlements of 200–300 inhabitants, and five or six groups of

Courtesy, The Bancroft Library

Leland Stanford Junior University, ca. 1891

farm buildings, along the whole distance of the five-hour railway trip (about 120 miles); there aren't any other "settlements." Reflexively, you recall Switzerland, where every fertile valley is filled with a town. You would expect that in the California climate, with such fantastically fertile soil—and especially near such a populous center as San Francisco and en route to another (the third by population) administrative center, Sacramento—there would be more. After all, there are not many valleys so fertile and with so favorable a climate; yet, although cultivated, it is nevertheless deserted. A year ago I happened to travel by coach for eight hours without stopping on the other, western, side of the bay. In all that huge area of rich fertile land, carefully fenced in for distances of twenty to thirty miles, I literally did not encounter anyone or anything except for a lone coach house and a Portuguese fishing hut nestled at the ocean's edge. When

I traveled by train across all of southern California to San Francisco I couldn't figure out where all the Golden State's inhabitants were hiding; what I could see might as well have been a desert, like the Sahara, with occasional small oases.

According to the results of my inquiries, the entire twenty miles of carefully fenced-in, empty land on the west side of the bay near San Francisco belongs to a California bank. When I asked an American camp keeper how much the bank asks for this land, his answer disconcerted me: $1,000 an acre! It's not surprising that it remains empty. Clearly the bank is saving it for future speculation.

In this regard it is not uninteresting to compare several figures. On territory three times smaller, the republic of Guatemala supports the same population as California: that is, about one-and-one-half million. It is curious that an entire quarter of this agricultural state's entire population is concentrated in the city of San Francisco and its suburbs. Incidentally, Guatemala is a comparatively wild and poor country with a primitive and, moreover, lazy population! With territory nine times smaller, our Bessarabia* supports the same one-and-a-half million population. The population density of Ekaterinoslav province outstrips California's by six times, that of Kovno province by ten. Tobolsk province is less densely populated, but nonetheless only four times less than the Golden State.

These are all significant facts, which can be explained only by the large capitalists' monopolies on land holdings and the land speculation that has become scandalous in proportion.

Most California capitalists did not make their millions in gold as is generally assumed, but precisely in land speculation. In essence, the mechanics are not terribly complicated. Just

---

* Bessarabia was a territory roughly equivalent to the present-day Moldavian republic of the USSR. Ekaterinoslav was in the southern steppes, Kovno in west Russia, and Tobolsk in Siberia.

recently we saw two prominent examples of how it works. One was in Los Angeles in southern California; the other was in Seattle in Washington State in the north. Large companies get their hands on big parcels of land, legally and illegally (for instance, buying up government land designated for settlers at $1.25 an acre through false agents). Once their right of ownership is guaranteed, a so-called "boom" is organized: which is to say, hullabaloo the world over, or the most brazen and unforgivable advertising campaign, launched in all forms. Huge amounts of money are spent on this. The press is bought and immigration recruiters are sent all over the world to look for fools. The area is advertised as paradise on earth, with gold mines, coal mines, forest and climate unlike anywhere else on earth; in a word, all you have to do is arrive and you'll become a millionaire.

And, wonder of wonders, as always, this brazen advertising campaign is amazingly successful. Contrary to Darwin, the number of gullible people in the world is clearly not diminishing. They come from all countries of the world and buy up the land in spite of the legendary prices. Then, of course, follows the natural reaction; hundreds and thousands are ruined; many lose the last pennies they've worked to save and treasured all their lives. Most of them return to the east and to Europe or enter the ranks of workers and offer their hands to these same companies in the already overflowing job market.

In this manner, the predators of capitalist feudalism kill two birds with one stone: On the one hand, they unburden the pockets of the immigrant; and on the other, they lower the working wage. I don't think that statistics for suicide and insanity among foreigners are worse anywhere than in San Francisco, that collection center for these recently well-to-do immigrants who have already been swindled by Americans only to have become part of the American working class.

In California, for every 300 healthy individuals there is one lunatic kept in an insane asylum. If you take into consideration those who do not end up in these asylums, the proportion, of course, is even more unfortunate. In New York, another state overflowing with foreigners, there is one for every 350. Generally, in western states where foreigners abound, the ratio is 1:400–1:600, while in southern states it is 1:1,000. The number of foreigners in California makes up one-third of the whole population, and this third yields two-thirds of the lunatics kept in asylums.

In spite of constant immigration from eastern states and Europe, the state's population is growing very slowly. Every day one or two trains packed with immigrants arrive in San Francisco, and so it continues the whole year round. During spring and summer months there are, of course, even more. But the simultaneous, and almost equivalent, movement out of the state explains the small increase. It is very, very difficult to find work, even for a true worker who has been accustomed to physical labor from youth and is skilled in a good trade. Work is inconsistent and unpredictable, which means that half the year you are forced to miss work and that, in actuality, the notorious good wage of $1–2 a day comes out to the same as European rates, particularly if you take the expensive cost of living into account.

As for intellectual occupations — they are impossible to find. California capitalists have an open aversion to any kind of scholarly or theoretical knowledge, and where you cannot possibly avoid it, they either give preference to practical workers who have mastered the business routine or reserve such positions as sinecures for their relatives. Concerning professional law, medicine, and the like, you could say that they don't exist in California. The local lawyers and doctors are simple tradespeople with ideas characteristic of the commercial and business class, and that level of education and morals. Anybody who knows the rudiments of reading and writing can become a lawyer or a doctor in the course of 3–18 months. Thus the competition is horrible and so unscrupulous that it is impossible to even speak of adaptability for someone with a European understanding of the professions.

San Francisco is the only city in America with a Russian colony, although a small one. This draws to California a fair number of homesick Russians who have been scattered individually in different states. Let this somewhat long digression serve as a warning to them, if only as a weak antidote to the "worldwide hullabaloo" produced with the mercantile aim of profit by Americans, a hullabaloo that reaches even Russia and tempts those who do not live so well in their homeland. The grass is always greener.

On Railroads and the Road to Sacramento

4

Sacramento, the Chinese, and Opium

But here is Sacramento. You approach it almost imperceptibly, because it is located in the same valley as San Francisco, at the Sacramento delta where the river flows into the bay, and thus is hidden by the surrounding suburban gardens. You cannot see the city until you actually enter it. It is not very different from other American provincial cities, which remind me a lot of our temporary fairground buildings. Straight, not-so-wide streets, arranged at right angles to each other, are lined with wooden barracks-like buildings put up for the purpose of displaying merchandise. Taste and comfort are certainly not the

Courtesy of the California State Library

Sixth Street, Sacramento

main concerns. Shops, colorful with merchandise and advertisements of all sorts, occupy the entire lower floors. Awnings, propped up by wooden poles along the length of the whole street to protect the merchandise from the sun, form something of a long gallery, interrupted only by cross-streets that are poorly "paved" with planks. This is the sidewalk. Above it, in several larger buildings, are second and third stories housing hotels, offices, studios, and so forth.

A horse-drawn tram runs along the middle of the street. This is the commercial center of the town. But there is not much commerce here. As the capital of the state and the residence of bureaucracy, Sacramento lives by red tape—that is, paper pushing, so called since all official papers in the states are written on paper that has red tape on one side.

And sure enough, after two business streets, we get into a completely different section of town, one occupied by bureaucrats. The streets here are wider, with trees planted on either side. In general they are somewhat similar to French city boulevards. It would be impossible to live here during the summer without some shade, because the heat can be unbearable. The houses are also built with summer in mind; they are small wooden cottages with porches half-covered in vines. Some of their facades face right onto the sidewalk, which now is a true open sidewalk. Other, more expensive ones are slightly removed and set amidst small gardens. The construction is even lighter than in San Francisco: The inhabitants spend the whole day outside, in the garden or on the porch, with the house serving just as a place for meals and as a nightly refuge. The streets are quite dirty and dusty in spite of watering.

Courtesy of the California State Library

Sacramento, 1880

Sacramento, the Chinese, and Opium

The city's main attraction is, of course, the capitol, where both houses of the state convene and all the offices are located. It cost the state a lot of money ($2.5 million), out of which only a small part of the allocated sum actually went to the building; the rest, as usual, lined the pockets of the builders and those responsible for overseeing and controlling the project. For the same reasons the city hall of San Francisco has cost around $5 million so far, has been under construction for about thirty years, and cannot seem to be completed! The residents are certain that no matter how much money is allocated, all of it will be stolen.

The capitol is built in the same style as the one in Washington; indeed, it is an exact replica. Most of the state capitols are built according to the same design; if you've seen one, you've seen them all. They remind me a lot of the central churches in our provincial capital cities: the same deserted square—the boulevard with crazily pruned trees that provide neither shade nor shelter, the same wide paths, rarely a bench, the same signs not to walk on the grass, the same large dome with porticoes and columns. It is exactly the same as the American parlor, where everything shines in gold and crystal, where an unusual cleanliness reigns, where the sun's rays are shut out so as not to spoil the carpet, where it is uncomfortable to sit down and impossible to pass through freely, where smoking is prohibited and you have to spit into your own handkerchief—where, in brief, the guests and the hosts alike feel utterly out of their element.

From the outside, the Sacramento capitol does not make any impression other than of massiveness. This is due largely to its dirtyish appearance and to the stucco that is crumbling in some spots. However, it is much better inside. Here, it is elegant and comfortable and, if you will, even beautiful. The space beneath the dome is not divided into levels, but left open, because the floor beneath it separating the stories is cut through by a large opening, fenced off by a low iron grille, so that the marble

Courtesy, The Bancroft Library

State Capitol Building, Sacramento

cluster of Queen Isabella, her husband, and Columbus, to whom Isabella is presenting her diamonds—a rather well executed group of statues presented to the people of California by some rich man—can be seen from above and below.

The chambers for both legislative houses are furnished elegantly and comfortably: each representative has a wonderful soft-velvet armchair and a fancy desk. The halls are covered with luxurious thick rugs and surrounded by colonnades in back of which runs something like a corridor, separated only by a heavy rich drapery. It gives the public and those who are not taking part in the debates, but don't want to leave the hall, the opportunity to feel a bit freer behind the scenes without bothering the speakers and listeners.

Near both halls is a most conveniently constructed library, which consists, for the most part, of books concerning politics and law. As in all American libraries, the visitor here is at complete liberty. Shelves filled with books classified by subjects replace catalogs. Anyone can freely climb the stairs to the galleries and rummage in the books as much as he wants; if he has any difficulty locating something he needs, he can ask the librarians, who are always very obliging.

The stairways and corridors of the capitol are decorated with decent oil paintings depicting scenes from the state's history. One of these paintings shows an emigrant wagon train from the Forties, when the Pacific Railroad did not yet exist and when pioneers had to cross the terrible barren deserts between the Rocky Mountains and the Sierra Nevada with oxen. The second shows the interior of a hut belonging to the first gold prospectors: A group of drunk gamblers sits around a table with cards and bottles, and, by the stove, one tries to melt his loot of gold dust in a metal spoon.

Besides the commercial and bureaucratic sections, there is a Chinese quarter located right by the dikes that protect the city from frequent floods—dikes whose construction and maintenance nearly bankrupted the city. This is, of course, the dirtiest, most stench-ridden and impoverished part of the city. It does not even consist of houses, but of mere huts and lean-tos that are plastered with long, vertical, red signs in Chinese.

These inhabitants of the Celestial Empire live in a far from celestial manner. Someone who has had occasion to peek at the midships of the German and English steamers that transport emigrants from Hamburg and Liverpool to New York will have some idea of how the Chinese live on shore. Imagine the lowest and smallest possible room, all the walls of which are hung from top to bottom with navy bunks. Each of these bunks is the apartment of a Chinese. The filth and stench are unbearable, especially at night, when all the lodgers gather and each lights his stinking opium pipe. And almost all of them smoke. How could you not smoke? The entire numerous Chinese population of California (about 100,000) is in the hands of three powerful

Chinese companies that merchandise their labor in a manner approaching slavery.

Let's say a certain capitalist needs 100 or 1,000 workers. He turns to one of these companies, which neatly provides him with the required number accompanied by their foreman, who is often the only one to speak English. The usual pay is $1 a day per head, paid directly to the company. The company feeds and clothes the workers itself with products shipped from China. Whether or not the Chinese worker smokes, he is obliged to pay for his daily portion of opium as well as for food, clothing, and other things; the cost of the opium is very high due to the steep tariff.

Having paid for his opium, how can he not smoke it—especially when everybody around him is smoking?! Almost

Courtesy of the California State Library

Late-19th-century underground opium den

half the daily wage—that is, about 50 cents—goes for opium. Add to that the amount deducted for the large bribes to American police, customs, and judicial authorities tied to the importation of this nominally forbidden ware, for the food provided by the company, for clothing, for the expenses of transporting this pariah from China and returning his bones in case of death, and what remains to the Chinese worker for his chain-gang labor? Yes, chain-gang labor and a chain-gang life, and no way out of it. He will be sure to take up smoking!

Opium smoking, along with morphine and cocaine addiction, etc., is spreading very rapidly among the white American population not only in California, but throughout the territory of the States. In San Francisco alone, according to customs records, 500,000 pounds of opium have been unloaded during the last eight years, and 50,000 of that during the first six months of last year alone. This is not to mention what has been illegally imported, for the contraband product is flourishing. Not only the Chinese companies but a significant share of California's politicos live off it as well.

For this reason alone, the Chinese immigration should be stopped and an effort should be made to remove the coolies already here. Public opinion in the state insistently demands this, and laws prohibiting the importation of Chinese are devised every year. But the American and especially the California plutocracy needs beasts of burden. (Without the Chinese competition, the white worker might be singing a different song.) Therefore, these laws meet the same fate as all laws that conflict with the interests of capital—either they are not implemented at all or they are circumvented.

The latter option is facilitated by the judicial-administrative machinery, which is entirely dependent upon these interests. One of the usual means is habeas corpus: that is, the right of every citizen (except in certain criminal indictments) to freedom from preliminary incarceration if he posts bail. In San Francisco they ironically call this the "habeas corpus factory," since the judges release the Chinese coolies by hundreds on the basis of their false claims to citizenship—claims whose lack of foundation is discovered only at the trial where the accused usually fails to appear. As for bail, it is always fictitious; in the end, it turns out that there is nobody from whom to collect it, and the Chinese remains at liberty.

As in San Francisco, in Sacramento a significant part of manufacturing and commercial operations is concentrated in the hands of Jews. On major Jewish holidays, San Francisco is reminiscent of our western Jewish cities. In Sacramento the firm Weinstock,

Courtesy of the California State Library

Weinstock, Lubin & Company Building, Sacramento

Lubin & Company amounts to something like the notorious Kannivershuala.* It is impossible to walk along the street without seeing this name dozens of times. It adorns all the cars of the horse-drawn tram, many wholesale warehouses, stores, banks, and land agencies. Messieurs Weinstock and Lubin emigrated from the Polish provinces to become stars of the first magnitude in California. The city and the county of Sacramento are simply their feudal holdings. Not only wholesale and bank commerce, but also huge parcels of land have turned up in their hands. Recently, along the lines of Baron Hirsch,** they have organized a Jewish agricultural colony on this land. As far as I could understand, patriotic and philanthropic feelings in this amazing plan are in absolute agreement with an American businessman's common sense. The Jewish emigrant receives a piece of land, a house, farming equipment, cattle, and even food prior to the first harvest. The plot is even transferred into his name, but is mortgaged by Messrs. Lubin and Weinstock until such time as the settler pays back its cost and all the capital that has been spent on him, along with moderate interest. If he doesn't make payment, the plot is returned to the original owner and the settler is allowed the right to find a more profitable application for his labor. The original landowner alone knows how much the land cost initially and the price for which he gave it over to the colonists. We Russians should be proud of such people who were born under the same sky as we.

---

* Phonetic translation from Russian of a probably German or Yiddish term—perhaps *keine verschollene*, or, loosely, "can't get rid of 'em."

** Baron Maurice de Hirsch was a German financier and philanthropist, founder of the Baron de Hirsch Fund for support of Jewish immigration to America from Russian and Romania. Hirsch was especially interested in establishing Jewish immigrants as farmers.

45

Sacramento, the Chinese, and Opium

5

Placerville, "Express," and Coal Kings

Because the track from San Francisco to Sacramento makes up part of the large Pacific Ocean railroad, trains move along it at substantial speeds. However, the secondary line by which we had to travel further to Placerville is quite bad. Without even mentioning the fact that on this line there is only one train a day, for which you have to wait a whole three hours in Sacramento, the track is so bad that the cars rock and shake as if they were on cobblestones. Because it is impossible to travel at the usual speed on this sort of track, the train goes only ten miles an hour, covering the short distance of 55 miles to

Placerville in over five hours. The cars are dirty, uncomfortable, dark, evidently reconstructed old cattle cars.

This secondary line abandoned its previous northeastward direction and turned straight west, perpendicular to the axis of the Sierra Nevada range. The slow pace gave us a better look at the surroundings. A feature of the Sierra Nevada range is that in spite of its great height, it does not make any particular impression as you approach it. This is due to the gradual rise in elevation. So, all the way from San Francisco we saw neither snowy nor even any significant peaks. Neither did we see any particularly picturesque landscapes.

As we approached Placerville, which is located at the very foot of the mountains, I asked (not without surprise): Where, after all, is this famous Sierra Nevada, whose sonorous name ("snow teeth") has been connected ever since elementary school with so much that was poetic and picturesque?

Everything we had seen over the course of these 55 miles was a hilly, rather wild, unpopulated area. There is only one settlement—Folsom City, with 1,200 inhabitants—the whole way. Here and there is an isolated farm or a group of Chinese lean-tos, however. Dug-up, broken-apart hills of red clay—evidence of the previous excitement of gold fever—pop up quite often, a depressing sight. Here and there a few Chinese in their blue shirts are still digging, preferring to earn that dollar a day outside their companies.

The American gold prospector considers it unprofitable to work in places that bring less than $3 a day. At one time this whole area was covered with splendid forests, but not even hoarfrost is left of them now. The vegetation is wretched: From tall weeds to wild bushes. In general, the area gives the impression of a recent battlefield on which the onslaught of artillery turned everything topsy-turvy.

We arrived at the Placerville station at dusk and traveled the quarter mile to town by cart, which dropped us off at the hotel

Courtesy of the El Dorado County Historical Museum

Placerville Depot

of a Mrs. Kiene. A Russian compatriot recommended this hotel to me; he recently left his young wife in San Francisco (neither of them knows a word of English) to travel to these parts. His wife was supposed to follow him shortly thereafter; and, in a letter, he gave her detailed instructions on how to travel. In part, they read: "When you arrive at the Placerville station beyond which the train does not go, tell the cart driver: 'To Mrs. Kiene's.' He will bring you to the hotel; the proprietress will seat you at a table and ask, 'What would you like? Lamb cutlets or some sausage?' And you say, 'Some sausage, Madame Kiene, some sausage.'"

Reading this letter, we automatically remembered the instructions. Following them exactly, we found ourselves at Mrs. Kiene's, an old lady of German descent who settled in this town when it was founded and has lived through all its memorable history, remaining loyal to it in spite of all the vicissitudes of fate.

Mrs. Kiene's hotel is somewhat peculiar. It is housed in a little old ramshackle hut on chicken legs, the type that probably made up the whole little town of "Hangtown" in bygone days; the name has since been changed to the more presentable Placerville ("town of gold deposits"). The little house is two-storied. Its entire first floor is right on the ground, occupied by one big, low-ceilinged room very similar to our cellars where workers entertain themselves with "liquor by the drink and take-out." On the left is a bar; behind it the shelves are filled with pitchers and bottles, and between them and the bar is the short, fat, good-natured, loquacious little Mrs. Kiene herself. Farther behind the bar on the same side you can see the sheltered passage to the second floor, and to the right, one after the other along the room, stand two big, long tables covered with clean dishes as old and peculiar as the proprietress herself. Yet despite the poverty and simplicity, the whole establishment has a tidy appearance.

The old lady greeted us cordially, not at all in the American style. She gave us the chance to wash up a bit, then immediately seated us at one of the large tables and treated us to her sausages and whatever else there was. All during supper she never stopped entertaining us with her interesting stories about the gold rush, which awakened half-forgotten scenes from Bret Harte in my memory. After all, it all happened either here—in this same establishment, before the eyes of this same woman, who was then young and beautiful—or nearby. Who knows? Maybe some heroines were based on her. At any rate, because of her beauty, which is still preserved in spite of her age, it is impossible that she was not, at that time, a participant in many escapades and perhaps the unwitting cause of more than one crime. Modesty held us back from this line of questioning.

Our hunger satisfied, we were led up the staircase, whose steps squealed plaintively beneath our feet, to the upper floor, consisting of a narrow little corridor onto which opened several doors to tiny bedrooms separated by wooden partitions. The walls of the closet assigned to us must have been covered with white canvas a long time ago in order to guide the water streaming through the roof somewhere other than onto the heads of the sleeping guests. The canvas, now yellowed, hung in blisters and was covered with outlines of the puddles and streams of water that had flowed over it.

The floor, it turned out, was built so that the most cautious step is louder than a drum or a microphone; the most minute

Courtesy of the El Dorado County Historical Museum

The Placer Hotel, Placerville, built in 1856 and owned by Mrs. Kiene

movement produced something along the lines of a camp alarm. You might think that the construction was specially built with medical considerations in mind.

The beds were even more interesting. Not only did they groan and whine piteously every time you turned over, but, worst of all, the mattresses resembled the Sierra Nevada with all its peaks, ravines, and valleys in miniature.

It is impossible not to dwell on these details, because Mrs. Kiene's hotel is its own sort of historical monument, a reliquary of past times. The newly rich adventurer-pioneers who patronized it during the gold rush were not at all particular about comfort; and then, when the mines ran out, the state of affairs in the town grew so rotten that there was no longer any means to repair things, and nobody for whom to fix them.

My traveling companion and I devoted the whole morning of the next day to a tour of the town—and to extracting our baggage from the claws of Wells & Fargo, the express company. Our Russian understanding of "express" is rather cloudy, because there is nothing like it in Russia or any neighboring countries. Nevertheless, in America it plays too evident a social role for me to remain silent about it. To begin with, the carter is called "express." Of course there are thousands of this type of express in every big city in the world. Sometimes these are poor souls who earn their living by transporting freight and baggage at their own risk. More frequently they are small entrepreneurs or companies who maintain a more or less substantial number of carts and horses. Such enterprise has not gone beyond this level in Russia, if you don't count transport bureaus.

It is another matter in America. Here, under the name of "Express Company," there are special firms that deal with transport, banking, and postal matters on a scale only a government could manage. Given the comparatively underdeveloped principles of government in general and government ownership in particular, nothing has prevented these companies from

Courtesy of the California State Library

monopolizing such important economic matters as the transport of packages, baggage, cargo and merchandise of all kinds and, to a degree, also letters and money. They have managed to make themselves so indispensable that whether you want to or not, you have to deal with them every step of the way. If you have to transport your baggage from one place to another in Russia or in Europe, you take the nearest carter; in America you have to telephone express, because the carter is too expensive—in San Francisco they charge $2.50 per trip plus $5 an hour. Carters are hired only for funerals, weddings, and other such extraordinary circumstances. Of course you can go out on the street and look for an independent carter who would perform the same service for $1, but that is still expensive if you don't have much baggage (and understandable, for he has to take only your things and cannot accept any less). And besides, it's a bother. It is much simpler and easier to call the express company, which will arrange all this for you at 25–50 cents per piece of baggage, depending upon the size. If you have to send your things to another city, not just in the States but also abroad, once again it is simplest of all to telephone express so as not to chase down a carter and accompany him to the station or port, where you must wait for a long time and maybe even lose a whole day.

Furthermore, the railroad companies have deals with the express companies, based on mutual concessions and favors. If, for example, you want to send a box containing foodstuffs as baggage or freight, the railroad will not take it, but instead sends you to the express company, which will accept everything. If you have to send a package to some city in the States or abroad and you go to the Post Office, in three cases out of four they will not accept it because its weight, dimensions, or packing are not in accordance with the postal regulations. If you call on express, they will come to your house and accept anything to send anywhere. If you need to send an important letter, whose contents you do not wish to become known to a curious postal clerk or your business competitor, again you must entrust it to express, which will surely deliver it and not divulge your secret.

The same goes for money; it will be delivered faster, no matter to whom or where, than if you send it through the bank or post. And all this happens decidedly without any long or tedious formalities. The agent who calls on you will give you a receipt on a scrap of paper; there's nothing more for you to worry about. Everything is done unbelievably simply, quickly, and accurately. It appears to be a golden institution, impossible not to envy.

In actual fact, this is not the case. At the time when there were many competing companies, maybe it was this way, but now the business has gone the way of all profitable businesses and has ended up in the hands of one enormous company, which, by legal and illegal means, has killed all its competitors and uses its monopoly in the most unscrupulous manner. Long years of experience, the selection of experienced and proven workers, and, most importantly, extraordinary investments of capital in the enterprise make new competition practically impossible.

And what would be the sense in competition! If people agreed to spend new millions on a parallel company, in the shortest possible period the old company would break them—either by lowering prices, or through recourse to its stable prior connections with railroads and steamships, and its experience; or, if that turned out to be impossible, it would consume them or swallow them into one even more voluminous business, forming a so-called "trust"—that is, a commercial-manufacturing combine. Ultimately, almost all branches of industry or commerce in the States have taken this shape and, for all intents and purposes, are monopolies. The high protective tariff that makes foreign competition impossible has been a particularly strong incentive for this tendency. Apart from branches of industry in which the States are safe from foreign competition due to soil, climate, and other local natural conditions, the branches of industry in which these trusts have sprung up solely because of the protective tariff number around a hundred. For interest's sake, here is a list of them:

> the coal mining trust, the trusts for manufacturing sharp iron tools, wire fencing, china, nuts and bolts, teakettles, shoes and boots, the trusts for producing borax, brooms, brushes, buttons, light bulbs, cartridges, castor oil, celluloid, cigarettes, condensed milk, smelted copper, copper sheeting, rope, dishes, cotton spinning, cottonseed oil, cotton thread, electrical appliances, envelopes, glass, pitchforks and shovels, fruit preserves, galvanized iron, gloves, agricultural harrows, scythes, door hinges, hardened filaments, lead, bootsoles, lime, flaxseed oil, lithographs, locomotives, marble, matches, moroccan leather, oat flour, oil cloth, paper bags, tar, mirrors, pocket knives, gunpowder, canned goods, wood pulp, rice, rubber, cash boxes, salt, sand, medical supplies, sandpaper, frames, saws, school books, school furniture, sewer pipes, shot, meat hooks, cast iron, tool handles, soap, soda water machines, sponges, starch, steel,

> rails, stoves, matting, steel girders, sugar, fuller's teasels, tin sheeting, headstones, trunks, metal pipe, typesetting, umbrellas, steam engines, wallpaper, clocks, wheels, whips and lashes, window glass, wire, wood screws, wool hats, wrapping paper, yellow pine.

And out of the myriad trusts that have arisen as a result of protective tariff and class legislation, these are only the hundred examples cited by Congressman DeWitt Warner.* Essentially, you could say that practically all manufacturing in the States has already become subject to monopoly, due either to the tariff or to natural circumstances. The goal of all these trusts is threefold:

1) To reduce production. The trust pays most of the plants the entire sum of their year's profit on the condition that they close their factories or reduce production to agreed-upon levels.

2) To extract from the consumer the highest possible prices they can pay for goods (all that traffic can bear) and in no case less than the amount of the protective tariff, that is from 25 percent to 200 or 300 percent.

3) To lower the working wage.

As for the means by which competitors are broken and forced to join the trust, in this regard the monopolists fear neither human nor divine law. Here anything goes: from all kinds of commercial, stock market, and financial tactics intended to ruin and crush the stubborn competitor to setting fire to or dynamiting his factory. Just recently there was a court case concerning a powerful water trust that had bribed people to burn and dynamite one stubborn independent plant. The perpetrators were caught redhanded at the scene of the crime

* Rep. James DeWitt Warner (D.–N.Y.) served in Congress 1891–95 and was president of the American Free Trade League 1905–9.

with solutions of phosphorus in carbon sulfide and hellish dynamite contraptions.

The meaning of these trusts for the consumer and production worker is best seen firsthand. For an example, let's take the coal-mining trust. In the sixth official yearly report filed by a labor commissioner for the Federal Government in Washington are a number of extremely interesting facts. The coal corporations gave this agent access to their records only on the condition that he would not name individual companies and mines in his official account, but rather designate them with numerals. He kept his word; 147 coal-mining enterprises in the States, as well as several foreign ones, are identified by numerals in his account. According to his research, it turns out that, taking into consideration wages for workers and administrators, rent, interest, insurance, deterioration of machinery and buildings—in a word, all possible expenses linked with the industry—the cost of one ton (2,000 English pounds) of coal in the United States equals 92 cents. According to the accounts of the railroads, the average cost for transport and delivery of coal to the consumer is 98 cents; thus coal delivered to the consumer's doorstep costs on average $1.90. However, according to this same report, the actual average price paid by the consumer for a ton is equivalent to $5.50, so that the monopolists' average profit consists of $3.60, or about 190 percent.

As far as the workers' pay goes, the average for the States is 60 cents per ton. According to the report, mine No. 9 pays 95 cents (maximum wage), No. 31 only 20 cents (minimum). In No. 9 the worker extracts an average of thirteen tons a week, which makes (assuming that this is a full-time job!) $12.35 a week. He works 1,400 feet underground, and out of these wages he has to pay for his own lamp oil and powder, as well as the blacksmith for repairing his tools. In No. 31 the worker extracts an average of sixty tons a week, working 900 feet under the earth's surface. The coal is filtered through a sieve; the workers do not receive anything for the fine dust that escapes the sieve, but this does not prevent mine No. 9 from selling this dust for $19,000 a year. No. 31 makes $1,750.

In mine No. 40 the worker can extract only eleven tons a week. This is the minimum amount of product produced by one man in the mines in the States. Work here goes on 2,000 feet beneath the earth's surface. In recent years the amount of coal produced annually in this mine was 28,000 tons, and the dust was sold for $6,000. This mine pays the worker 75 cents per ton, which comes to $8.25 a week for full-time work. It costs the worker 11 cents a week for tool repair, 20 cents for oil, and 70 cents for powder, leaving him net earnings of $7.25 a week. On average, workers have work only five days a week, which reduces their net earnings to $5. And the fact that, due to the high price of food, the worker can acquire no more for these five dollars than he would in England for five shillings, or in Germany for five marks, makes it clear to the reader what this famous protection "of labor(!)" the American capitalists hide behind leads to. It doesn't hurt to note for comparison's sake that according to official accounting, the average cost of coal production in the United States is 92 cents per ton; in Canada, $1.40; in England, $1.15; and in general for all of the European continent, 72 cents per ton.

Nevertheless the coal kings, still dissatisfied, demand a higher tariff on coal. In this manner a few monopolists comprise all manufacturing and industry in the States. Even the free citizen, as both producer and consumer, has to pay these companies and corporations dearly. Every branch has its own king, upon whose arbitrary rule everything depends. There are kings of sugar (Spreckles), railroads (Jay Gould, Stanford), kerosene, telegraph, steel works (Carnegie), and more. In a word, it's really a feudal system. Incidentally, our Russian bread manufacturers, sugar factory owners, and oil producers have to some extent already given the Russian public a similar lesson. Their corporations represent on a small scale what is happening on a large scale in the States.

Wells & Fargo are the kings of express. They have offices not only in every state with a population worth speaking about, but also overseas; it's no more or less than a great empire. God forbid that you find yourself in their hands; nevertheless, whether you like it or not you end up in their hands almost every day.

And they fleece you. Once I had to send a manuscript notebook to Europe through them. For postage I paid $5. In this particular instance we were charged $3.75 in Placerville for transport of a trunk containing food worth a couple of dollars (which the railroad will not accept as baggage) from San Francisco; that means about 50 percent *ad valorem* for a relatively negligible distance.

It's an absolute nuisance to receive any sort of packages from Europe. When the foreign postal service delivers to New York, it gives them to customs. The whole mechanism in customs is designed so that the addressee himself cannot possibly receive them. It is necessary to hire a special customs broker even if the addressee himself lives in New York. If you live in some other city, then the broker turns up of his own accord and informs you that he has arranged the business with the package for you and offers his bill of charge, which far exceeds the cost of the object itself. But that's not all. He turns the package over to Wells Fargo and they cruelly fleece you once again. In most cases, it is more sensible not to accept your property than to pay the high duty, the broker's charge, and the express fee; I have done that on more than one occasion.

6

A Wrong Turn Leads to Mosquitos, California

Placerville, a small town of $2\frac{1}{2}$ thousand inhabitants, is laid out like our Russian villages, in one long street at the bottom of a small ravine. Behind the houses on one side of the street stretches an uninterrupted range of hills covered with green forest, resembling the edges of a ravine, where flat-leaf and coniferous trees are mixed half and half. These hills, along with the blossoming orchards, drown out the wooden cottages and give the town a rather pleasant, picturesque, even dandyish look, especially on this sunny summer morning. Midway down the street is the obligatory commercial quarter with several shops and taverns standing beneath ordinary wooden signs. There are also several small stone buildings. This is all you can say about it without exaggeration. However, in one of the many brochures published by California capitalists in the interest of attracting immigrants, this is what it says:

> Placerville, the county capital, is located at 38° 43' N and 120° 47' W and is 1,800 feet above sea level. The population numbers 3,000. Its community, climate, wonderful school buildings, comfortable family life, and huge business section are constant themes for local writers. The town is conveniently located near the center of the county; the court buildings, a huge hospital, and a model farm are located here. All the county officials live here. The foundry and machine factory in this town are well known throughout the whole area for their excellent products. All the machinery used to dig the Big Tunnel to the north of town, work on which is progressing unusually quickly,

Courtesy of the El Dorado County Historical Museum

Main Street looking east—Placerville, ca. 1891

> came from this factory. The factory is managed by Mr. William Morey, a steel worker and machinist with thirty years of experience. Placerville is endowed with two large school buildings, a first-class Academy [probably something analogous to the Smorgon academy in our western region, where bears are trained], and four marvelous churches, which are filled with attentive churchgoers on Sundays. The business section is comprised of all trades and professions known to active city communities. The surroundings are very thickly settled: four people per square kilometer! What Placerville needs is a fruit-drying and canning factory and a wool-spinning plant. It is certain that both these enterprises would be profitable.

This is the usual tone of such promotional advertising literature. Alas, we did not see any of this in Placerville; we saw neither the first-class Academy nor the rich churches, schools, or factories; if they really exist, then it must be in microscopic form.

I think that every one of our own one-horse towns could write something no less boastful if they wanted to imitate the enterprising Americans.

The most valuable thing in Placerville is the earth upon which it is built. In this earth there is a lot of natural and even more spilled gold. Several capitalists have offered the town a significant sum of money for permission to dig up the main street and pan it for gold.

With the exception of several Jewish and American shopkeepers, the inhabitants are, for the most part, unsuccessful former gold prospectors who had to forget about the gold and take up the more reliable and profitable activities of orchard growing and cattle raising. They are kind, simplehearted, and talkative folk. Any passerby will tell you all there is to know about his town, his neighbors, and himself, just like a Frenchman; in the end you'll be thankful for any excuse to get away from him. Because travelers here are rare, our appearance on the street aroused intense curiosity on the part of the locals. As we walked along the shoddy plank sidewalks (which were sometimes absent for whole sections of town, forcing us to crawl through the mud), we saw a Chinese laundress receive gold sand as payment for washing. As you see, the old coin, the bit (i.e. a pinch of gold equal to 12½ cents) has not yet gone out of fashion here.

Several miles from Placerville is a small settlement called Coloma, a place where the first California gold was found by a certain James Marshall. He is buried there right on his former homestead, and appreciative Californians have erected a modest monument at his gravesite.

Our route did not lie in this direction, however, so we were not able to visit Coloma. After we saw the town and stored all our baggage with Mrs. Kiene, we filled our pockets with provisions and set off on foot to the mountains. It was ten o'clock in the morning. The previous evening and throughout the night it had rained, but now the sun shone brightly from a cloudless sky and warmed everything. Here and there puddles remained, but thanks to the road's sharp incline, the mud did not interfere with our excursion. We were to cover about ten miles; we marched merrily along the red clay, jumping streams as we encountered them and feeling the way horses must when their harnesses are removed and they are set free in the field.

Each to his own; but city life, with all the conveniences of civilization, is its own sort of heavy harness, very pleasant to part with—at least temporarily. That especially goes for San Francisco, where life is distinctly void of spiritual satisfaction, where it is possible to live for years without meeting a single person who is interested in anything other than the cost of the soap he produces. Granted, soap is a useful product; however, soap in your mouth, nose, ears, eyes, soap behind the collar and in your soul itself, soap everywhere—you have to agree! It is an exasperating business!

Just as the great Sierra Nevada has been out of sight all the way to Placerville, you will not see it here either. Slopes covered with green forest and broken by ravines—that is the whole panorama. The stony carriage road cuts around the ditches in big zigzags, crossing from one slope to another. Over the course of the whole ten miles there are five or six isolated farmhouses.

Courtesy of the El Dorado County Historical Museum

Marshall's Monument at Coloma

In one spot, the most scenic one, a hanging bridge spans a deep rock ravine through which a powerful mountain stream races, jumping from cliff to cliff, foaming and raging. It is the South Fork of the American River, which flows into the Sacramento. Right on the bank is a pretty, newly painted and fenced-in farmhouse on 160 acres of land, recently purchased by its current owner for $1,000.

Punctuated by small breaks, the road stretches through forest. At first the trees are small and flat-leafed. Then come large lumber stands, where conifers increasingly predominate. This forest covers huge areas and has not yet been heavily exploited because there are no convenient routes for this purpose. As a matter of fact, rich companies already have their hands on a significant chunk of it; they have bought up government land designated for settlers through false agents, and have already arranged to build a railroad and hydraulic devices for floating the lumber.

The Americans, just like we Russians, are rapacious with their forests. If this sort of land mismanagement is not brought to a halt in time, sad consequences await us: The rivers will get shallower, there will be droughts and worse.

Huge amounts of timber are brought from Washington State by sea; but in the Sierra Nevada there is only small-scale lumbering done by poor people who cannot find more profitable work. Once they have found the appropriate tree, they fell it and make shingles out of it. Locally the price for a large load is $5; for the same load delivered to Placerville the going rate is $10. The poor men who do this earn about $2.50–3.00 a day, while the man with a pair of horses and conveyance earns $5 a day. On winter days when there is nothing to do on the farm, farmers don't disdain this income. Making shingles and panning for gold in the ravines provide constant and reliable support during hard times for anybody who wants to work. In some spots there are small sawmills. Several locals guide plank rafts down the American River, which is a pretty dangerous business because the furious current frequently carries away the daredevils and smashes them on the rocks.

For me, this forest was the most engrossing object of our entire trip. As one who was born and grew up in the forests of Russia, and knows all the Russian species and kinds of trees, I find it strange and exciting to be in a forest where everything is new and unfamiliar, where at every step there is a new surprise whose name and characteristics I can only guess. Several years ago when I was walking around the outlying areas of New York, I was struck by the rich variety of utterly unfamiliar deciduous trees. Here in the Sierra Nevada there is a new, particularly localized flora that has very little in common with the flora of the eastern states. I have already mentioned the California oak in the valleys (*Quercus chrysolepsis*). You encounter it frequently here, too, but there are also five or six other varieties of oak that do not look much like each other. Among them is our ordinary European oak. (Here it is called

Courtesy of the El Dorado County Historical Museum

Small sawmill, Placerville, ca. 1891

the mountain oak.) Other than these two, the so-called live oak (*Quercus agrifolia*) is very widespread in the Sierra forests. There have been up to fifty varieties of oaks counted in America.

There are two species among the special Sierran flat-leafed flora that in particular call attention to themselves: the madrone (*Arbutus menziesii*) is a small but very beautiful tree that looks like the magnolia, with smooth brick-red bark, fat shiny leaves, and a beautiful flower. Its fruit is an edible red berry. The manzanita (*Arctostaphylos*) is a large, well-proportioned bush of unusual beauty, with smooth reddish-brown bark and small, fleshy, round, shiny leaves that more resemble coral reefs on the bottom of the ocean than they do any land plant. Its fruit is also an edible berry, but it tastes very sour. Neither of these species loses its leaves in winter; both stay green the whole year round. As for usefulness, neither one yields anything but good firewood. Manzanita has a very bright white flame and thus served us well all during our travels. A campfire made from branches of Manzanita replaces candles and lanterns and is inferior only to electricity.

As far as coniferous trees go, they are more varied here than in any other place I have ever been in the world. But I would rather tell about them later.

Along the way the only animals we encountered were several squirrels, along with one example of the spotted skunk (*Mephitis mephitica*) which, not wanting to become saturated for months with its horrible odor, we didn't follow. The bounty for the pelt of this latter animal, which destroys domestic fowl, is 50 cents; for a squirrel, 25 cents; and for a wolf or a jackal, $5. They say that an enterprising local Yankee was inspired by this to raise wolves.

In one place we were supposed to turn off the big road, which leads to the town of Georgetown, onto a cart track. We missed the turn and got lost, only to discover our error quite late. We had to retrace several miles and did not feel up to reaching our destination that evening, and besides, a light rain had started to fall again; so we ended up staying at the farm of one Mr. Dickerson.

Mr. Dickerson was a prosperous farmer, with a very patriarchal, respectable appearance. He seemed to be at least 60. He had long gray hair, a big gray beard, an unusually puritan, reserved-serious appearance, and an intelligent penetrating gaze which it was impossible not to read as "You don't have to struggle to account for yourselves, because I can see right off the bat what's up and what sort of people you are!"

Courtesy of the El Dorado County Historical Museum

The trail to Mosquitos, and a California oak

Dickerson has a very large family consisting of several grown sons, of whom two are married and live with their wives and children under the same roof as he. He himself does not work anymore and only supervises, in fact checks from time to time more than anything. His personal labor has been reduced to fulfilling the uncomplicated responsibilities of the local postmaster. Two times a week, one of his grandsons is sent on foot or horseback to Placerville for the mail; the letters and newspapers he brings back are distributed by the local farmers who pass through.

The family lives in a small, already decrepit house of several rooms. The front room has a huge fireplace in which large logs were flaming as we entered. The old man sat in his armchair at the hearth, smoking a short little pipe. One daughter-in-law was reading a book, while the children quietly played in the corner. On the walls, along with two or three lithographs, hung various farm implements. The whole room, papered with old newspapers, looked poor but homey.

Although Dickerson does not formally keep a hotel, he offers shelter to all travelers who pass through. Breakfast and dinner cost 25 cents; lodging also costs 25 cents. When he found out that we hadn't eaten supper, he looked at his reading daughter-in-law, who closed her book and energetically set the table in the middle of the room with two places for us, as the family themselves had recently eaten.

Supper was farm-style: It consisted of the customary Turkish beans with pork and boiled potatoes, white bread, milk, and stewed apples, with a big cup of black coffee. There were no drinks. The master of the house spoke very little during supper; the other family members did not say a word. The old man limited himself to well-considered and careful answers to our questions, especially when we started talking about the availability of government plots and the price of land in general. Businesslike, Anglo-Saxon coldness permeated his every sentence. However, we were able to find out that he came from the eastern states and had arrived in California during the first gold rush. After unsuccessful prospecting, he began to prefer farming—which is why he settled here in Mosquitos, where he was able to obtain a free government plot for himself.

The young daughter-in-law took up her book again, and one of the sons took us into the neighboring room, furnished with pretensions to city comfort. Besides two beds with fresh linen and curtains (for protection from mosquitoes) there were a mirror, several paintings and photographs, bookshelves, and various knickknacks on shelved tables. A new house, much larger and hardly different from urban middle-class cottages, stood a hundred paces from the old house. Not far from it was the school attended by the local farmers' children. We had a chance to see this school subsequently, so I will tell about it later.

Just as all the farmers here, Dickerson does not actually work the land; that is, he does not plant grain. Orchard-growing and cattle-raising are the main profitable activities. He, as the wealthiest farmer for miles around, can serve as an example of what level of prosperity a diligent, sober, and wise pioneer, for whom a bird in the hand is worth two in the bush, can attain during the course of his life, without gold or commercial speculation, simply by using the strength of his own hands.

I don't know the absolute size of Dickerson's current holdings. I know only that, other than his own plot of 160 acres of free land and another 160 so-called "preemption" (obtained from the government for $1.25 an acre), each of his sons has similar neighboring plots. Besides land, Dickerson has several hundred head of horned cattle and several dozen horses. An irrigation canal, which now brings some profit and promises to be more profitable when the surrounding land is more thickly settled, is also part of his holdings.

7

In Hill Farm Country

From Mosquitos the road traveled upwards by way of the same unending half-flatleaf, half-coniferous forest, burned in places, skirting large ravines and crossing small mountain streams. The forest quiet was broken only infrequently by the murmuring of water or a frightened wild dove or squirrel. There were practically no small birds to be seen. Contrary to our expectations we walked right until sunset, when, to our delight, we found ourselves on a big green sloping forest clearing surrounded by a fence, on the opposite side of which we could see two farm buildings. This is what is known as Soapweed.

Soapweed got its name from a special local strain of large lilies (*Chlorogalum pomeridiamum*), which end in a cluster of beautiful miniature lily flowers and have a large bulb. This bulb, when rubbed in water, yields soapsuds. In earlier times the gold prospectors frequently used it instead of soap and, out of gratitude, named this place after the plant.

Intending to spend the summer in the mountains and not knowing the best way to arrange this, we had put an ad detailing our needs in several local newspapers a week or two before our departure. In response we received several dozen letters with all sorts of suggestions, one of them written in spry Spencer calligraphy and signed by a Mrs. Golden. The author of this letter offered us, for a very reasonable price, room and board in a comfortable apartment with a small family at the elevation of 3,000 feet, in a forested, healthful area covered with mountain streams in which you can swim and fish for trout. In addition the letter mentioned that there were harmoniums and violins in the house, which, like everything else, would be available for our use.

One talkative old man in Placerville gave a very flattering report, ending with the comment that the Goldens never came to town with an empty wagon; they always brought enough goods with them to pay for their purchases! Old Dickerson, assuming that we knew her well, remarked with an ironic smile that Mrs. Golden had gotten married again. As amusing as it was to hear all this, these laconic remarks gave us no idea about the family of which we intended to become temporary members; thus, it was not without curiosity that we entered her home.

The Golden family, it turned out, consisted of three or, if you will, four people. The actual head of the family—the pioneer, gold prospector, and farmer, Mr. Golden—had died several years ago; he drowned floating timber down the American River. A man who preferred, according to reports from his neighbors, to live by his wits rather than by hard work, he was a resourceful speculator for whom his farm—or farms (besides Soapweed, he had another in the valley)—served only as residences.

When Golden died, he left an old widow and two sons behind him. Both farms now belong to the old woman. One son is the head of the main lower farm; the other, who just got married, has herded all the cattle up here for summer pasture and will spend his summer honeymoon with his mother and young wife.

The old mother, who still bears the traces of her former beauty, is tall, straight, and shapely, although her hair is gray and her face covered with wrinkles; she is now no longer Mrs. Golden, but Mrs. Markell; for after a long common-law marriage with her neighbor (also as old as she) that began soon after the death of her husband, she registered her official marriage to him. But, for certain family reasons they do not live together.

In the eastern states, Mrs. Markell was a seamstress; she came here with her husband during the gold rush. Right up to this day she dresses nicely and has not abandoned her corset.

Courtesy of Lolita Mattei

Soapweed, 1891

But what is most remarkable about her is her small, mischievous, dancing blue eyes. If you look at them you'll say to yourself: "This one is not to be trusted!"

Further observations absolutely justified that first impression. During the long hours we sometimes had to sit with her, what brilliant plans and tempting suggestions did she not develop before our eyes! Everything led up to the fact that she wanted to sell us one of her farms at a profit. This would allow her, you see, the chance to move to San Francisco. When this scheme found no takers, she announced her willingness to relieve us from all the bother of city housekeeping and make herself something along the lines of our *major domo* for appropriate recompense.

And so forth, and so forth. The problem was that the old woman's affairs were in bad shape. The farms were mortgaged and overmortgaged and she wanted to live a bit in her old age. In the forest, you're among wolves; what kind of life is that?

It wasn't the first time in the States that I had met this sort of old woman, overflowing with passion to enjoy her last remaining days. Usually as a person ages, his or her interest in life in general, and particularly in its material temptations, weakens. With the instinctive knowledge that the fateful end is near, the fleeting and transitory qualities of the self—the very center of gravity of life's interests—somehow involuntarily transfer in some form or another to the Great Whole, the approach to and merging with which of the human *I* is the basis for all religions, all poetry and philosophy. The most despairing egoists begin to care for their children, or, if they don't have them, for other beings who need guardians and protection. The most jaded skeptics and materialists are taken with mysticism of one sort or another. For both types, a need for peace and solitude is born, a tendency toward the contemplative life.

Here, generation after generation has been raised on the principle of "everybody for himself and the devil take the hindmost." So it is not surprising that in this classic country of individualism and egoism, more than anywhere else, there are vast numbers of severe pathological cases who remain true to their principles right to the grave. Even with one foot in the grave, they have time neither for relatives, nor friends, nor for humanity in general; they ignore their own children, regarding them simply as a burden. They are the center of the world. For them the world and humankind exist only to the extent that these are necessary for personal pleasure or satisfaction. They look upon the services and sacrifices of those around them as something natural, owed them; and they are exasperated and enraged when they encounter rebuke or refusal.

Most often, although hardly exclusively, these types are found among the local rich people. Supported by the omnipotence of their capital, like a Grecian sponge, like cancerous tumors, they mercilessly suck all the nourishing juices from the surrounding environment into themselves; without remorse, they sacrifice everything and everybody to their monstrous egoism. They do not know pangs of conscience. Old age does not cure them; on the contrary, they then lower themselves to all possible means to satisfy their animal instincts, buying everything that it is possible to buy for money. And what can't you buy in the States?!

Jay Gould, the railroad king who died recently, was one of these types; so was the steel king Carnegie, and so were dozens of other rich men whom I happen to know personally. One of them, moreover one of the most decent among them, recently absolutely stumped me with a statement of this sort: "You are a strange people, you Russians. Wherever you look, you always have a principle. You are absolute children! After all it seems clear as day that there is only one principle on earth: 'How much?!'"

Alas, the whole nation is raised on this principle. It is the main and most essential strand of people's lives. All the rest is absolute hypocrisy.

In Hill Farm Country

There's nothing new under the sun. Egotistic maniacs have been known in all epochs and all nations. The reader will say, "Take the contemporary Russian Razuvaevs.*" Yes, of course; but the question here concerns the stage of development. I can claim only that in the States this type has already been accepted widely and deeply. That is, on the one hand it has been developed too much, as much as if razuvaevism were to become one of the essential elements of our national character; on the other hand it has gone very deep and been perfected to the point of absurdity. In the worst case, the Russian skinflint, with his defects, his Achilles heel, can be gotten to if you try skillfully. For one thing, he is far from occupying the leading role in society, and thus is vulnerable to appeals to his ambition. The wealthy American with the strength of his riches, in and of themselves, already stands at the very top of the social order; he is already an aristocrat, a powerful magnate, a king idolized by everybody, in whose hands are concentrated all the political and economic attributes of power, all of Jupiter's thunder and lightning bolts.

For another thing, the Russian miser can be religious, or at least is not estranged from the church. You cannot get to the American "big-bug,"** as they call them here, on this account. He knows and recognizes only arithmetic: "How much?" Yes, and if there were a tidy little million or two for old Mrs. Markell, she would make herself heard. Luckily, God doesn't always give horns to butting cows.

Mrs. Markell does not work any more; the young daughter-in-law, Mrs. Golden, does work and, as it turns out, was the author of the letter. Mrs. Golden is a young, shapely woman of 25, healthy and strong, although slighted by nature when it

---

* Prototypical money-grubbers from 19th-century Russian literature.

** "Bigwig," perhaps?

comes to beauty. Her face is lumpy and pimply, which completely spoils your impression. She is lively, doesn't have to hunt for words, and is at the same time not stupid and not without a good measure of tact. Although she grew up in the country not far from Coloma on her father's farm and has not once in her life been farther than Placerville, you don't notice her provinciality at all. The only child in her family, she is somewhat spoiled. When she has to work, she is a master of all trades, and when she can slack off, she turns into a silent log only dynamite could move. On these occasions, she can lie and sleep several days in a row, waking up only to accept food prepared by somebody else. However, when it is *necessary* to work, she will cook dinner in $\frac{1}{2}$–1 hour, bake bread, set and clear the table, wash and put away the dishes. And she does this three times a day: at six o'clock in the morning breakfast is prepared; at twelve, lunch; and at six in the evening, dinner—each indistinguishable from the other, each requiring the stove to be fired up again. In the intervals between this kitchen bustle, she manages to clean the rooms, milk the cows, look after the chickens, and more. All this takes her surprisingly little time; she still finds time to read a 10-cent novel and play the violin for an hour to the accompaniment of her husband, whom she has taught to play the harmonium by ear.

Mrs. Golden sings a little, and not at all badly, reading the notes quite rapidly. Her general education is equivalent to what our third- or fourth-form gymnasium students would have, if you excluded foreign languages and the entire theoretical-philosophical side of education from their training. Incidentally, her education is higher than average for a farmer's daughter, as she was an only child and had a mother who . . . * What differentiates her even more strongly from our gymnasium students

* Several words are illegible in the original manuscript.

and young ladies is the absence of any trace of romanticism, cloudy impulse, or exaltation. She has no interest in any sort of abstract subjects or questions. She possesses practicality, realism, and the healthy striving of a healthy body to chat, enjoy herself, and dance—especially to dance. In this respect, in the actual art of performance, and her passion for it, she can compete only with her husband, who is transformed beyond recognition in dancing society. From a healthy, red-cheeked, heavy, lazy fellow he turns into a genuine salon cavalier who could easily dance the whole night away.

The farm itself consists of two buildings: a house and a hayloft, both in pitiful shape. The house is a small, completely decrepit, rotting, ramshackle wooden building sort of like the ones that can sometimes be found in the lanes of our suburbs where the petty bourgeois live. It is encircled by a covered porch and essentially consists of two rooms separated by curtains. On the right is a clean room, furnished in the urban style like Dickerson's. Drawings and photographs decorate the bare walls; the small windows are hung with muslin curtains. In one corner is a bed with a mosquito net; in the other, a harmonium, a couple of tables covered with knickknacks, two or three wooden chairs; those are its furnishings. If there had also been several potted geraniums in the windows, you would have thought you had moved in with some petty-bourgeois woman in a provincial Russian town.

The other front room serves as a dining room. Here, as at Dickerson's, there is a huge open fireplace built of natural uncut stone. At the window there is a shelf, and in the middle of the room is a long table. The ceilings are low, the walls are papered with old newspapers torn in half. Under the eaves in the attic there are two minuscule bedrooms; since the roof is full of holes, you have to set up all sorts of contraptions to protect yourself from the rain. Luckily it doesn't rain very often.

The other building, the hay loft, serves all purposes. Not

only is hay stored here, but also several head of cattle as well as wagons and farm tools are sheltered within, and there is a place for pigs underneath. Although new, it leans severely to one side under the weight of last year's snow because it was poorly and quickly built. Barring active intervention, it threatens to fall down completely; but at the moment, nobody is thinking of intervening.

The whole farm consists of 160 acres, if you don't count the adjoining 160 acres the old woman took with the intent to resell. Of these, only the fifteen around the house are fenced in. These fifteen acres consist of sloping forest glade, in the middle of which runs a small stream flooding a large part of it. The glade is filled with a meadow covered with sedge. It would not be difficult to grow a marvelous grass here, if you were to dig a few ditches. However, neither Golden the father nor Golden the son ever concerned themselves with this. Right near the house on one side there are several dozen fruit trees that have also been let go, and on the other side a small garden, a large part of which is taken up by potatoes.

Turning the earth in this garden and planting the potatoes and cabbage were the only work we saw done by Golden, the son, over the course of two months; but here, too, he didn't manage without hired help. Moreover, two or three times a week he goes to Placerville without any important business, just to spend time. What was said about him in Placerville—that he doesn't ever appear there emptyhanded—was only a compliment, or perhaps ironic. Not once did we see him take something there to sell.

The farm's only income comes from its cattle. But even this is done in a very idiosyncratic way here. According to state law, other owners' cattle are prohibited only from your fenced-in areas. Such fenced-in places count for only a few drops in this unending sea of virgin wood. Hence the whole forest, private and government, is open pastureland. Not only the locals take advantage of this; cattle farmers who live far away in the valley drive thousands of head of cattle up here for the summer months. Both the farm cattle and the cattle from far away are branded. There is absolutely no supervision of them. As soon as the snow melts, the cattle are driven into the forest, to be rounded up only a week or two before the new snow. The cattleherd's only work is this search for his animals, who have dispersed for dozens of miles in the thick forest.

The locals manage this seemingly impossible task amazingly well. On horseback with lassos in hand, a knowledge of the local area, and the help of two or three herd dogs, they round up all their cattle in several days together with the herd's summer

Courtesy of the El Dorado County Historical Museum

Cattle drive, Placerville country, ca. 1891

increase. Of course a certain percentage is lost, most frequently falling victim to wolves and the local California mountain lion; but this percentage is so insignificant that it isn't worth maintaining special herders to avoid the losses. For the most part the animals are horned, but there are some horses, and also pigs fattened on acorns for the summer. Of course, in this system the whole milk yield is lost, but because milk production seems too painstaking for the local farmer, he keeps only a few cows at home for his own use. With few exceptions he is careless with this milk. What hasn't been drunk and has gone sour is all thrown out to the chickens, cats, and pigs. In general Americans do not consume sour milk or cream. They don't know how to make cheese, either. In all of California only one kind of cheese is produced, and it is of very low quality.

8

A Country Dance

At this elevation (3,000 ft.), snowcover lasts only a short time—from two to four weeks. The farmer's main concern is to somehow feed his animals during this short time. In order to do this, somehow or other you have to store hay during the summer. The best farmers plant clover, timothy, and the like. Bad ones, like Golden, get away with sedge. Nobody plants grains. They plant garden vegetables late and harvest them at the end of August, so the farmers actually have to buy them in town. The same goes with fruit. In general, except for pork, game, chickens and eggs, potatoes, and milk, everything else has to be purchased. The town merchants willingly give credit until autumn, that is, until the harvest or cattle auctions. The prices for bought produce, especially on credit, are high, and the prices for selling produce depend upon the good will of the large wholesale buyers and bigwigs, who have taken care of this already in the very best way. Thus even the good, diligent farmer is glad in autumn if he is able to cover the debts he has accrued over the course of a year. As young Golden says, you can exist here one way or another, but no more. Because he is not satisfied with this and wants to *make money,* he looks hopefully to new, open places in the north and intends to move to Washington State.

During our stay with the young Goldens, Mrs. Crawford, Mrs. Golden's mother, came to visit; we spent several pleasurable days in her company. I will permit myself to dwell on her, because she also represents a type of American woman, unfortunately of an outmoded generation. She is a tall, shapely, thinnish woman of about 40 with a direct, open gaze and an intelligent, kind expression. Good spirits and energy permeate her whole figure. Her earnest face smiles at you cordially all during the conversation. She is very active; her hands are never idle, but this doesn't prevent her from having serious conversations. She dresses very simply, without the slightest pretensions to youth or inclusion in a class to which, according to her means, she doesn't actually belong. All this together with her modesty and kindness makes her immediately attractive. Further acquaintance opens a whole gulf between her and young American women. The contrast is striking and far from favorable to the younger generation.

In spite of her intellectual development and rigorous education, unusual for a California farmwoman (she is a former Boston schoolteacher), and in spite of her age, Mrs. Crawford is very inquisitive and never misses a chance to learn something new. The young American woman has nothing to learn; she knows everything. But what struck me most of all about Mrs. Crawford was her deep interest in abstract, general, philosophical questions. In this sort of American woman, sober realism and unusual practicality are surprisingly combined with an impulse to look more deeply and widely at the surrounding world, with a taste for pure philosophical theories and generalizations. No less surprising is the frankness and directness with which she expresses her views, the courage of her convictions. When the topic of conversation for a young American woman is not the weather, but rather such subjects, I can never believe that she says what she thinks, because five minutes later, in conversation with my neighbor who insists on a diametrically opposite position, she will be equally comfortable agreeing with him. Either she doesn't have any of her own opinions—there is only, "Whatever you wish, just so I please you?!"—or, if she does, then she will not voice them.

According to Americans, it does not pay to say everything one thinks. The best of them are silent, but will not contradict anything. Their conversation is a sort of careful exploration and banal assenting. They are inspired to great heights by everything that pleases you, horrified and indignant at that which evokes your disapproval, and so forth.

Mrs. Crawford is religious in the best sense of the word. Her faith is an expression of her own spiritual world and is not constricted by any dogmatic or sectarian traditions. There is nothing contrived or rigid about her, nothing that isn't the product of her own intellectual work. This is a woman who, throughout her life, not only never stops working with her hands and by the sweat of her brow to earn a living, but also never stops thinking; she is a well-rounded person with broad, courageous views on things, the sort of person one feels to be conspicuously absent in contemporary America.

Her past is very unfortunate. A native Bostonian, she was a public schoolteacher in her youth. When she married a poor man, they thought they would try their luck in California, which, at the time, excited the whole world. They arrived here as gold prospectors and within a year or two had been so unlucky that they prepared to return to the east. On the eve of their departure, her husband took his pickaxe and shovel to try one more spot he was reluctant to abandon without examining. Toward evening he returned with $800 in gold. Their departure was postponed. Further work in the same spot brought him several thousand, with which he started a fruit farm near Coloma. They continue to live on this farm now. The most important item they produce is peaches. With constant work, extreme economy, and good harvests they hardly make ends meet because of exploitation by wholesalers and high railroad tariffs.

"Why don't the orchard growers in your area organize their own company, which would have its own canning factory, its own warehouses, its own agents in the east?" I asked her.

Courtesy of the El Dorado County Historical Museum

Carriage and driver, Placerville area, ca. 1891

"It would be very good—we would avoid the constraints and blackmail of the wholesale companies—but we would all have to agree on it."

"So, why not agree?!"

She smiled and, looking intently at me, said: "Why? Just imagine. It seems simple, but the main difficulty lies precisely in this. It is hard for people to agree among themselves even if the issue clearly concerns their mutual interests."

Yes, people everywhere will be people. I have always been amazed by Americans' skill at organizing themselves quickly and at their ability to simply and practically manage their business together. But evidently there is a limit to this skill. The difference from us Russians is only a matter of degree.

During the time that we stayed with the Golden family, we were able to attend a country party, which I cannot resist describing in more detail. One of the locals of the fairer sex thought up the idea of organizing monthly socials for the young people. No sooner said than done. Once a month from Saturday to Sunday there is a gathering of the local maidens and cavaliers who spend the whole night, each time in a difference place, dancing and singing and courting. This time the party was to be at Mosquitos in the schoolbuilding, five miles away. Our hosts, certainly not excepting the old woman, decided to go, and offered to take us with them.

Fascinated by the prospect of catching a glimpse of this side of farm life, we willingly accepted the invitation. We set off at about seven o'clock in the evening, at dusk. As we entered the forest it became completely dark; we had to grope our way, as it were, and proceed slowly in the areas where there were steep ravines. For the most part, the road sloped in the direction of the ravines, and many times we almost broke our necks. I won't even mention the suffering we experienced along the way. At each jolt our heads bumped against the sides and roof of the carriage, which left tender bruises for a whole week. I don't think the injuries would have been more considerable if we had been rolled down these hills in a closed barrel. American carriages are built for the comfort of horses, not of people. They are very light, but extremely uncomfortable.

But where there's a will there's a way. At the risk of falling in battle, we reached our destination by ten o'clock. We were saved only by our driver, by Mr. Golden's thorough knowledge of the road and locale. When we reached the school we found a dozen similar chariots already there. There was no entrance, so both woman and men had to begin their *partie de plaisir* by climbing over the fence. In order to keep animals from coming into the school yard, no gate or door had been built; but there was something like a staircase which, if you had some gymnastic skill, you could climb to reach the top of the fence, and from there, in the same manner, you could descend. Both the children and the teacher complete this at least twice a day.

We crossed the yard and reached a newish, recently finished, not yet painted school building. The building is wooden, of course, but spacious, and consists of one large room. The doors were propped open, and several cavaliers were cooling off and smoking on the porch. Several steps and we found ourselves in the school itself, which had been turned into a dance hall for the evening. The schoolbenches were cleared away, and some were piled one on top of the other in the corner, forming a significant platform on which stood three musicians: two fiddles and a flute.

The rest of the benches were pushed against the walls, providing an opportunity for those who were not dancing to sit down. In order to sit down or stand up you had to warn the others who were sitting, lest the equilibrium be suddenly disrupted and the public either tossed upwards or thrown downwards, depending on the circumstances. Lighting consisted of a half-dozen candles stuck in bottles attached to the walls like a candelabra.

There were about thirty people, equal numbers of men and women. Old men and women and children huddled near the walls, some sitting, some standing because there was no place to sit. The young people of both sexes promenaded back and forth in pairs. The dancers were dressed simply, but city-style: The men wore black frock-coats; the women, light print dresses.

Only one or two maidens stood out for their elegant costumes. One of them was in a white muslin dress trimmed, not untastefully, with lace and ribbons. Someone introduced her to me and we started talking. She immediately let me know that she was not local but "from over the mountains" (in other words, from the neighboring state of Nevada), that she was a city girl

Courtesy of the El Dorado County Historical Museum

Mosquitos schoolbuilding, ca. 1891

who had ended up at this party by chance. Obviously she did not want us to mistake her for a farm girl. And with that dress and figure, and by the color of her face, she really did not look like these muscular, tanned country girls, full of health and strength. She was the only one of those present whom it was impossible not to call beautiful; but it was a hothouse, city beauty. She was short and had a pale, thin little face with a fairly intelligent expression and black, expressive eyes. She also didn't dance badly, unlike the others, and carried herself very sweetly and freely.

Alas, the rest, not excluding the teacher herself, were not exceptional for their beauty. Conversation with them was a bit difficult. If clumsily, they most diligently whirled through waltzes and schottisches. (In the States this is what they call the old English "country dance"; something much like our *"Miatelitsa"*—alternating quadrilles and the Virginia reel.) They whirled, sweated, and panted, as if hurrying to make up for lost time. They were dressed simply, without pretensions to any sort of fashion, for the most part in light print dresses. Among them there were one or two rich ones, daughters of local cattle farmers with whose hand and heart a lucky suitor could receive "the half of the hogs."

As for the cavaliers, with only a few exceptions (including, of course, our host), their frock-coats fit them very poorly, and in spite of their energetic determination to overcome all obstacles, they danced even worse than the ladies. One young man just didn't know what to do with his long muscular arms and his even longer legs. The girls pushed and pulled him pitilessly in one direction and the other like some inanimate object. He was a classic country bumpkin, of elemental strength, able to roll logs as if they were light as a feather; but in the dance hall he found himself in a very difficult situation. He obediently and goodnaturedly went where he was pushed, changing direction only when he was nudged again. His feet somehow inevitably got tangled with the remotest of surrounding objects, stepped on toes, and became caught up in the folds of dresses; and his outstretched, long hands grabbed two or three women instead of one.

There were also other, even more interesting, types. Especially memorable to me was one fellow of 28, a tall brunet with powerful muscles and huge hands. His sparkling black eyes, expressing limitless resolve and energy, looked wildly and severely from under somewhat craggy black eyebrows. His awful, hypnotizing gaze together with his motionless physiognomy told you that he might do anything. You felt involuntarily terrified by this glance and could not stand it for longer than several seconds. I would not like to meet him face to face in the forest. He is one of those legendary heroes who effortlessly holds up and robs a whole train.

The music was impossibly harsh. The two fiddles and the flute were not in tune with each other; they squealed and whined pitilessly, and the first fiddle, from the height of his improvised platform, commanded the dances in a loud voice as if a whole division was parading before him. I could not help but think of our own village musicians. Taking into account all their imperfections, they are, nevertheless, artists in comparison with these. In general, the impression they made was quite primitive. Indian war dances would probably produce a similar result. Neither the sounds nor the faces fit in with the figures of the quadrille and their costumes. A campfire and Indian war songs would have been more appropriate.

In such circumstances at home, we talk, make noise, gesticulate, and laugh. Here, everything happens absolutely silently with a gloomy seriousness, as if it were a serious business. Each person volunteers his or her contribution for lighting and music, and everybody brings some sort of sweet dessert. During the intervals between dances, the public drinks lemonade that one of the cavaliers prepares right there in a metal bucket, mixing water, sugar, and lemon juice with a big stick. Because there are no cups, the lemonade is served in old fruit tins; it is drunk with sweet cakes. There are no drinks or snacks as we know them.

After the dances there was singing, but I didn't hear it; not wanting to spend a sleepless night, I made my way to our conveyance, wrapped myself in a blanket, and slept until sunrise, when my companions returned for the trip back.

95

A Country Dance

9

In the Scarred Forest Primeval

In all, we lived with the Golden family only the two weeks or so needed to orient ourselves. By that time, on our recommendation, another lodger had arrived from San Francisco; thus, by subletting our quarters, we could leave the farm without breaking our terms and set ourselves up in the woods, which was more in conformity with our preferences and our plans. For this, one-half mile from the farm, right on the irrigation canal, in the virgin forest, we built a dugout with our own hands and covered it with branches from the Canadian spruce (*Picea abies*). These branches are shaped like ostrich feathers, which couldn't have been more perfect for this purpose. The dugout turned out something like a garden summerhouse, quite pretty and comfortable. Inside we improvised two beds from thin shavings covered with small branches of the same spruce; in the middle of the red clay wall we made a large stove, Russian style, where we could keep a fire going safely all night. Although it was June, the nights were cool and the fire was hardly unnecessary.

My traveling companion was also Russian, and although he was born somewhere in the wilds of Vologda province, he grew up in Moscow and, as you would expect of a city dweller, was comically helpless in the mountains and forest. Without even mentioning the fact that he had difficulty distinguishing a pine from an oak, his imagination constructed fantastic fears and dangers every step of the way. He was particularly disturbed by air currents in our den, so he plugged the chinks to stop the cross draft and made all sorts of contraptions to protect from dampness and the possibility of "catching" rheumatism and the like. I explained the absurdity of his fears in vain; neither explanations, nor exhortations, nor jokes—nothing helped.

Wild animals were another bogeyman. The first few nights he did not sleep at all and kept two fires going—one in the stove, the other at the entrance to our dwelling. The latter was intended to keep mountain lions, wolves, and coyotes (*Canis latrans*) at a respectable distance.

I can't say that I slept well myself these first nights. The forest is full of life and the strangest sounds at night. Some kind of unusually stubborn bird squawked the whole night somewhere nearby. This short, piercing cry, repeated every second without respite, continued until morning. Every once in a while coyotes howled somewhere; sometimes a mountain lion roared; but not one of these sounds affects my nerves in the same way as the wail of a wildcat. This wail sounds not at all like a beast. It is a virtually human and, moreover, female cry, the cry of a woman who is extremely terrified. It is something supremely primitive and tremendous. When I heard this cry for the first time, I was so deceived that I took a gun, and, bumping my head, ran to the farm absolutely sure that something horrible had befallen Mrs. Markell, who was staying there alone that night.

Yet in spite of all that night music, living and wandering through these forests is just as safe as walking in your own garden. The strongest of the animals, the California mountain lion, is in actuality not at all terrifying. It is about as big as a St. Bernard, but is very cowardly and never attacks humans. Wolves and jackals don't attack either, not even in winter. The forest is filled with pigs and horned cattle, so there is food for all these predators at will and they are never hungry. This condition, of course, plays no small role in their peaceful relations with humans. People who have lived here for 15–20 years do not remember any instances when wild animals have threatened or harmed humans.

The most unpleasant inhabitant of the western forests and plains (although far from as dangerous as we are accustomed to think) is the rattlesnake. Even this creature avoids human beings and does not attack of its own accord, but limits itself to self-protection. However, in several places there are so many of them that it is impossible to avoid chance encounters. Remnants of dry skin on the tail after several sheddings form a shaker or rattle, which produces a rather loud noise whenever it is moved. This allows one to determine that a snake is present some distance away and to avoid a meeting.

Unfortunately, in August these snakes become blind, for some reason. In this state, it is easier to step on them unexpectedly, which sometimes happens during evenings or nights on the roads. They like to crawl out from the mountains and ravines and warm themselves on the road dust heated by the sun. The snake's attacks and attempted bites are not always successful;

a number of "favorable" conditions must coincide. Even when it bites, the snake does not always manage to secrete its venom into the wound. For this reason alone, dangerous bites are rare. In case of a bite, after sucking out the venom and cauterization, the usual American treatment consists of whiskey in enormous doses, as much as a person can drink. Rattlesnake venom is heart poison—it paralyzes the heart—so any means of stimulating heart activity is a good antidote. Californians have become so accustomed to their rattlers that they pay no more attention to them than we pay our less-dangerous snakes in Russia. Here even children combat them successfully. In any event, over the course of our two months' wanderings here we did not encounter a single one.

Another serious and dangerous predator, depicted in the State seal, is the so-called grizzly bear (*Ursus horribilis*); at one time these bears filled the mountains and forests of the Sierra Nevada, but now their numbers have been decimated; you can encounter one only in the zoo, and even then it is very rare.

Soon after we moved to the forest, we had a little adventure, thanks to which my Russian friend acquired a certain amount of notoriety among the neighbors. As a result of some complicated meteorological considerations, he preferred to sleep with his head toward the wide-open entrance to our dwelling. The dugout was not very big, his body was very long, and the bed was fairly high; thus his head almost stuck out under the overhang.

For some reason, on this occasion the fire at the entrance had not been lit. The full moon, looking down from the starry heavens, poured its bright silver light over the tall pines and firs, with their dark green foliage and yellow, silver, and reddish trunks casting fantastic shadows on the ground. The forest is magical on such nights; all you want to do is sit and admire it. For a long time, you don't feel like sleeping; then drowsiness creeps up surreptitiously. For a long time, you are in a transitory state where sleep and waking, reality and fantasy merge into one, complementing one another. The quiet is extraordinary, majestic. Both beasts and birds are silent. Even the wind has ceased and no longer rocks the Canadian fir's long mossy branches. Among them in the dark greenery, stars hang in garlands and clusters just like wax candles on a Christmas tree.

For a long time we didn't sleep. I sat at the entrance to our den at first, and then lay down on my improvised bed and continued to admire the moonlit night. My companion constantly tossed and turned, now sighing, now muttering something to himself. Evidently his fantasy was more far-fetched than usual, and dream visions of enemies poured over him. He called for me frequently, fearing that I would fall asleep and leave him alone with his fears. If a branch or pinecone fell, a bat or night bird flew by, he called me:

"Do you hear that?! . . . What is it? . . . "

I answered at first, but then fell asleep—I don't know for how long. I was awakened by two revolver shots, one rapidly following the other. This time it was I who asked: "What's going on?! . . . "

"'What's going on!' . . . You sleep fine with your head toward the wall. But the coyotes almost had a bite of us!"

"How could that be?"

"Well, it could, I assure you. If I had kept my eyes closed a minute longer, I might have been without my nose. Forgive me, but just now—right there at my head—there was a whole pack of coyotes. When I shot at them, they ran off into the bushes."

As he was saying this, he gathered the tables, chairs, and all of our makeshift furniture to make a sturdy barricade at the head of his bed.

The next day we told the neighboring farmers about this event and provoked universal, Homeric laughter. It turned out that our poor Don Quixote had not done battle with coyotes, but with their dogs, which habitually take the liberty of making night visits to every camp, treating themselves to thrown-away leftover food.

But, the hero of this adventure did not believe it. He stood his ground firmly and ever since has carefully barricaded his nose every evening.

According to old-timers' stories, the forest surrounding us, in which we lived for about six weeks and which we crisscrossed, carrying guns, walking along the edge and through the middle for the distance of a good ten miles, is hardly what it had been when white men first arrived here. When Indians, who lived by hunting, populated these areas, the forest was so clear that you could see a deer a mile away. For a hunter this is, of course, a great advantage. Now, because of frequent forest fires and felled

Courtesy, The Bancroft Library

Under 'Lover's Leap,' Placerville Road, near Placerville, ca. 1891 trees, the powerful timber forest is mixed with small and tenacious undergrowth. Forest fires fairly often devastate it for entire miles; alas, they are not only caused by carelessness with fire. The cattle farmers set fires on purpose in order to extend the pasturelands and improve the quality of the grass. An unseemly undergrowth of manzanita or varieties of prickly blackthorn soon appears on burned and cleared places. There is no supervision or control of this forest, no limit to a rapaciousness that has no respect for anybody's best interest and has only one goal: to obtain a quick and easy personal profit.

Of the large trees, the most valuable one here is the so-called sugar pine (*Pinus lambertiana*), which has a powerful, well-balanced, mast-like trunk, often with quite a large girth, and grayish bark. On places that have been scorched you can often find an oozing sugary area that looks like white gum. This appearance is what gives the tree its name. The locals use the gum as a light laxative. The sugar pine is excellent building material: It splits easily and evenly and thus is used to make boards and shingles.

The yellow pine (*Pinus ponderosa*) is likewise very widespread. It falls distinctly behind the former as building material; it is not as even, and the color of its trunk is very similar to our Russian pine. It is very pitchy and could yield a large amount of turpentine.

Besides these two species you frequently find the California yew (*Taxus brevifolia*), a tree related to the conifers; instead of a pinecone, however, its fruit is a berry notable for its marvelous elasticity—the Indians used it to make bows. It is quite pretty and looks like our firs, with the difference that its needles are a lighter green. Of the rest of the conifers that make up this forest, I will mention the Canadian spruce (*Picea abies*), a particular species of cedar; and the red pine (*Abies nobilis*), which is widespread throughout America and is a generally used construction material.

In the Scarred Forest Primeval

Not far from us there is an interesting little spot—Soapweed Canyon. Our den, for all intents and purposes, stands at the canyon's edge, but from here we can see only a sloping incline covered with forest and underbrush. When you descend it about a thousand paces and walk two hundred or so more through the underbrush of common forest hazel, live oak, and madrone, you discover that at the bottom of this wide, sloping ravine there is another, steep and precipitous, with almost perpendicular walls of red clay through which naked cliffs show in several places. Above, the tall forest obscures all but a narrow band of visible sky; below roar the falling cascades of the mountain stream. It is a naturally gloomy, wild, joyless spot. But as you look more closely at its torn shores, at the multitude of huge trees that have been uprooted and thrown here and there, at the chaotic, completely out-of-place piles of stones, you realize that nature alone could not have created anything like it, that she had some help here from a whole horde of cyclones. Everything has been left topsy-turvy, as if devils had played leapfrog. If I had to paint the scenery for the last scenes of *Faust*, I could not have found anything more appropriate. Anybody who likes powerful sensations should climb down into this ravine on a moonlit night and listen to the wildcat's hellish concert.

They say that faith moves mountains. I don't know about faith, but passion for gold does move them, and Soapweed Canyon can serve as a graphic example. All the destruction I have just described, all that inhuman work, was done by gold prospectors; not only did they turn over every pebble in this ravine and each grain of sand three times, but with the help of the so-called hydraulic method they actually relocated whole mountains from one place to another. Because the hydraulic method for mining gold was invented here and, for the time being, is used only here, I think it is not inappropriate to say a few words about it.

Here, just as everywhere else, washing gold sand began with the most primitive method: that is, a gold-prospecting pan, now used only for scouting to determine how much gold the sand contains. This pan is in size and shape something like a metal wash basin. When the gold prospector sets off to scout, he usually takes only a pick, a shovel, and this pan. Above all he needs to know how to find a place where he can be certain of the presence of gold; without this knowledge he can pan to the end of his days and not find a grain.

Gold traces are found mainly in ancient riverbeds where rivers no longer flow. As for this particular area, it is assumed that there was a river here in prehistoric times, now christened the Stanislaus River and now, of course, no longer existing. The gold is contained in the old bed of this river, which consists of

Courtesy of the El Dorado County Historical Museum

Hydraulic mining, Placerville area, ca. 1891

so-called grit or gravel—that is, small stones mixed with sand—in the riverbed deposited directly on top of so-called bedrock, the rock layer several meters below the current surface. Thus there is no point in looking for gold anywhere above or below this level of gravel. (It is nearly impossible to look lower because the bedrock is a solid rock layer). It seemed to me that in this case the gravel layer was more likely a glacial moraine than an old riverbed. At any rate, having found this layer the gold prospector, using his pick and shovel, fills his pan with it and, climbing down to the river, submerges it in water. By shaking and rocking the pan, he allows the flowing water to carry away the sand and pebbles until the black magnetite sand, heaviest by specific gravity, remains at the bottom. In it, it is easy to distinguish grains of gold and, with a subsequent more-careful rinsing, to separate one from the other. If there are five cents of gold in a pan of gravel, the spot is already considered sufficiently profitable to work.

The so-called "cradle" or "swing," still used often by Chinese, is already a significant improvement. It is a small wooden box, the upper, movable part of which has a bottom with holes. The gravel is placed in this part. When this part is shaken and rocked, the water carries the fine sand through the perforated bottom, which, however, holds back the stones. The latter are removed by hand; the fine sand containing gold enters the lower, inclined part of the box; its bottom has horizontal, low wooden barriers behind which the gold collects because of its weight. The lighter sand is carried away with the water.

Further development of the method consists of building sluices—long wooden boxes or troughs with low horizontal barriers for gold. Gravel is thrown in by shovel at the very end of the sluice. The large stones are held by a coarse grating and discarded. The smaller ones, together with sand, are carried the entire length of the box by the water. The gold settles behind the barriers, where mercury is sometimes poured in order to dissolve the minute gold particles. This method is still used in Siberia.

Manual excavation of the gold-bearing layer—removing by hand all the thick layers of earth covering it, transporting the sluice, and so forth—requires an enormous quantity of arduous labor. The use of this method is possible only in very rich deposits. To the extent that California deposits have gotten poorer and been exhausted, it has become necessary to devise easier and cheaper methods for washing. Without a doubt, the hydraulic method is one of them. With this method, the washing takes place in the same sluices, but the destruction of the rock layer happens not by hand but by means of water, in the following manner:

Somewhere at a considerable height above the river, lake, or other source, the necessary volume of water is diverted through sheet-iron pipes. If the waterpipe encounters a stretch of elevated terrain along the way, it is not routed through tunnels, which would be too costly, but simply thrown across hills and ridges, on the assumption that the siphon effect will work. Once the waterpipe has been brought to the point of exploitation, it is divided into the necessary number of branches, each of which is provided with something like a large fire nozzle. This nozzle is sometimes manipulated simply by hand; sometimes it is put on wheels so that the stream of water can be directed at will. Because of the huge difference in elevation of the two ends of the pipe, the water leaves the spout under such terrific pressure that not only could you kill a man with it, but, by directing it at the rock layers designated for destruction, you can reduce and scatter them with extraordinary ease. Everything that is washed away crumbles and tumbles down into the sluices that stand ready, and washes of its own accord. In this manner the labor of several people replaces the grueling labor of several hundred workers; whole mountains are washed and carried away, and the poorest deposits yield a rich profit.

In the Scarred Forest Primeval

The pressure in the lower parts of the pipe can sometimes be so great that the pipe sweats on its exterior—that is, the water seeps through the pores of the sheet iron. Amazingly the iron from which the pipes are made is itself no thicker than an average book cover, and only a little thicker than the sheetmetal used to make stovepipe.

Several years ago a mining engineer was ordered by our Ministry of Crown Properties to go to California in order to study this method on location, with the intention of using it in the Siberian deposits that belong to this ministry. The engineer came on a lavish expense account and studied the situation, but attempts to use the method in Siberian deposits, while costly, were not successful. As far as I can recall, the pipes ordered were expensive, thick-walled, and made of cast iron, which of course did not withstand the high pressure. During my stay in

Courtesy, The Bancroft Library

Hydraulic desolation near Dutch Flat, El Dorado County, ca. 1891

California, another Russian mining engineer, V.S. Reutovskii, has visited the California gold mines with the same goal—to get acquainted with the hydraulic method on a practical basis. Let's hope that this time things will go better and the former crude mistakes—which confirm our saying—"In every wise man there is a bit of a fool"—will not be repeated. Is it not indeed amazing that the ignorant American gold prospector-practitioner invented and successfully uses this impossibly simple method, which a whole board of our scientific engineers not only could not think up themselves, but could not even copy intelligently! Just think, what is all this science for, anyway!

The sole inconvenience of the hydraulic method is that destroyed mountains are washed away in the form of sand and clay and deposited in fertile valleys, which renders them useless from the agricultural point of view. Also in this manner, rivers become shallow and even blocked up. This condition has given rise to a strong movement of protest on the part of the agricultural population in the nearby valleys of California, and it was the reason for passing a law that prohibits use of the hydraulic method in the state. Incidentally, recently there has been strong agitation to repeal this prohibition, and it seems it will be repealed. The gold prospectors and the farmers have reached a compromise that requires the former to maintain the masses of sand and clay in the mountains by means of artificial dams.

All these inconveniences may be crucial for the grape, peach, and orange plantations in California, but they are of no significance in Siberia, especially in mountainous areas where it is impossible to even think of agriculture and you could not block or dry up a river by any means. If part of the Siberian mountains is carried into the northern tundra, the tundra will sooner gain than lose. Moreover, wide use of the hydraulic method would exponentially increase the amount of gold currently mined there.

10

Cranks, Princes, and Land-grabbers

Farmers like Dickerson and Golden are exceptions here in the mountains. Most of the farm population in the mountainous areas of Washington, Oregon, and California is represented by a certain class of Americans who belong to two types found throughout America: old bachelors and so-called "cranks." The word "crank" is derived from the same root as the German *krank*, or sick, but Americans give it the sense of a particular mental derangement. In Russian, this word can be best translated by the expression "touched," or "not all there."

But the reader shouldn't think that American cranks are really

crazy. To understand the true sense of the word you have to take into consideration the general unhealthily crude and narrowly materialistic character of American life. From the point of view of this bourgeois materialism, with which the "healthy" majority is saturated, each person for whom the saying, "man does not live by bread alone," makes sense—each person who has something on his mind other than plans for profit—is considered "touched." It doesn't matter whether this "something" is an original political, social, philosophical, or religious idea, only whether it is incompatible with generally accepted beliefs of the majority. In all the spiritual manifestations of human life, the "healthy" majority maintains itself by adhering to an established routine, an established catechism, justifying and respecting originality and energy only when they are directed toward increasing material wealth. Popular opinion brands anybody who deviates from this—anybody who expresses other strivings and, in one way or another, displays his original inner personality to the detriment of material interests—with the half-condescending, half-mocking term, "crank".

From the point of view of the American majority, I fear that our entire Russian intelligentsia—all our public figures, writers, and thinkers (excepting, of course, those who know how to make money even in these professions)—would be considered cranks. It goes without saying that this applies to L.N. Tolstoy and his followers. With all due respect for Tolstoy's person and talent, I have to say that the only thing that saves his popularity here is his Count's title, without which, alas, his reputation would run into trouble. Americans are poor judges when it comes to art and moral teachings. The Russian reader, of course, may shrug his shoulders and doubt the justice of my words. But I will firmly hold my own and tell him one of the thousands of little incidents I know that characterize the weakness for the aristocratic that is typical of democratic and republican America.

Sometime recently, during the English Prince George's visit

to the eastern states, there was a rumor in the San Francisco newspapers about his probable intention to visit the west as well. At this time a certain unknown young man was staying in one of the city's aristocratic hotels. The Negro elevator attendant, who had once seen the prince, mistook the young man for him. Struck by the resemblance while taking the new arrival to his floor, he called him "Your Highness." The people in the elevator heard this and raised the alarm throughout the whole hotel.

"Prince George is in the Palace Hotel!"

Everybody wanted to see the famous guest; everybody wanted to speak to him, but the menfolk did not know how to approach him.

"Good morning, Your Highness!" The ladies constantly scurried around him and dropped their handkerchiefs and handbags and were beside themselves with joy when he politely picked up and returned the intentionally dropped object. It was a chance to become acquainted.

"How kind you are, Your Highness!"

In half an hour the whole city was on its feet and newspaper reporters had already besieged the guest.

"They say that you are Prince George: Is this true?" asked one of the reporters.

"Well, if you put the question so directly," answered the unknown fellow, "then there's nothing for me to do but answer in the negative. I am not Prince George, but a traveling salesman from a soap factory in the east. But I am very sorry that you are destroying the illusion, not because I was pleased to bear the mistaken title, 'Your Highness,' but because all these people here were so sincerely and deeply happy. I didn't object, as I thought: 'Why not give them something to enjoy, when it doesn't cost me anything!' Yes, with your impertinent question you have deprived the hotel guests of great pleasure."

Our titled and dissipated guardsmen hardly realize the

marvelous careers they could have in this greatest of republics. The cranks are not crazy. They are the only healthy element in an ocean of "operators" of every sort and description. They are the salt and hope of the American earth.

Of course most cranks struggle in the ranks of the many progressive parties, like the nationalist followers of Bellamy, the advocates of the Single Tax Movement founded by Henry George, Christian Socialists and other Socialist factions, the Temperance Party, and so forth. But many don't have the strength or the desire to participate in such struggles. When they don't find contentment among people, they run to the mountains and forests and there live the lives of anarchists. In most cases they are bachelors or widowers. To them can be added other bachelors who for one reason or another have not been lucky in life, who have not been able to build their own nests in a civilized way and have given up everything in disgust.

As I have already said, most of the farm population in mountainous areas of the west consists of these sorts of bachelor-anarchists. You don't have to go far to find examples. Half a mile away from us there are two separate farms, one of which belongs to Mr. Cook, the other to Mr. Markell.

Mr. Cook is a small, thin man, the sort of whom we say: What is there for his soul to hang onto? He is 60 years old, and gray not only silvers his head but comes out strongly in his short, sparse, sandy-colored beard. We visited him many times and always found him working, dressed in threadbare work clothes—a wool flannel shirt with canvas trousers* and a jacket still bearing the traces of their former blue color.

It's remarkable how workers all over the world like that blue color. Beginning with the blue shirts of our Great Russian peasants and the famous French blue blouse, not only all of

---

* Russel meant Levi's.

working-class America, but even Chinese and Japanese coolies on the Sandwich Islands clearly prefer this color. Never did we see Mr. Cook in his black holiday finery with a white starched shirt, which he showed us, not without pride, among many such things kept in a large wooden trunk. Nor did we see the top hat; but we did see a photograph of him in all those fine vestments. The picture had been taken many years ago, when he was still a harness maker in the east. Having arrived here to look for gold, and not finding it, he exhausted all his savings and then chose the blessed lot of a farmer. That was seven years before I saw him. With one hundred dollars in his pocket and one horse he took a free government plot of 160 acres covered with large timber. For the first year he loaned the horse to a neighbor because he had neither a plow nor food for it, and, with energy customary only for an American, he began to work.

Courtesy of the El Dorado County Historical Museum

Farmhouse, Placerville area, ca. 1891

This pioneer activity in the virgin forest would have seemed beyond the strength of any other harness maker (and an old man to boot). But Mr. Cook did not consider whether it was within his strength or not. He felled huge trees, cut them up and split them, built a fence, rooted out the stumps, dug ditches, plowed, planted, and scythed, and, to crown it all, without any help he built for himself, with his hands alone, a marvelous log cabin with two spacious rooms.

In a word, this small, thin, little old man accomplished an unbelievable, superhuman task. Now he has a large potato field, a meadow planted in clover, several hundred fruit trees, several longhorn cattle, three or four horses and sixty pigs. He works tirelessly from dawn until dusk and does everything himself, alone. As an example to his neighbors, he milks his cows and makes butter to sell. He asked us how to make Swiss cheese, but it turned out to be too complicated for a small farm. Besides butter, he sells potatoes, pigs, chickens, eggs, and the like in town. He takes care of his fruit trees like a mother caring for small children. The lower parts of the trunks are carefully wrapped with rags so that the cats won't use them to sharpen their claws. He passionately loves his whole farm, but these trees are the particular object of his love; no matter what time of day you arrived, without fail he would take you around the orchard, stopping at each tree to look at it lovingly and tell its biography. The old fellow has worked so much on them that he has put his whole soul into them. They are his children and will soon guarantee him a comfortable existence in reward for his painstaking care.

Mr. Cook can serve as an example of what can be attained by one man with his bare hands, as it were, if he works with energy and sobriety. Whom is the old man working for? It's not good in California to be poor, but with his limited needs he could surely earn his living in an easier way—by harness making, at any rate—in the nearest town. He was never married and has no children. His niece works at a post office somewhere in Washington, and somewhere else he has a nephew. He plans to invite the nephew to live with him when the farm gets going. That is one of his probable motives. Otherwise, he loves nature and independence and would not trade his farm for the most luxurious, idle, and senseless vegetating in some Palace Hotel or other in San Francisco, which serves as the residence for those California millionaires so rich in money and poor in spirit.

His neighbor, Markell, also an old man and also solitary in spite of his legal connection with old lady Golden, is an absolutely different type. His farm is an empty place. It consists of a small forest meadow overgrown with bad natural grass, in the middle of which stands a dilapidated ramshackle hut. There is not a tree or field or any trace of farming activity. Several head of cattle and pigs wandering freely in the forest seem to constitute his entire visible property. He himself is a tall old man, stooped with age, with a big gray beard and wise eyes. He is by nature a gold prospector. Farming is disagreeable to him and he doesn't hide it. He lives here, firstly, because you have to live somewhere, and, secondly, because he doesn't lose hope that the right to mine the surrounding mountains (which he says are filled with gold) with the hydraulic method will be restored.

Markell has had money more than once, and more than once he has squandered it in risky gold-producing enterprises. He invested his most recent money in building a long canal that he had wanted to use to begin hydraulic work. But just then the above-mentioned law was passed and the old man's capital was sunk in the canal, which brings almost no income, although it exists and is maintained. He speculates with whatever pennies remain and subsists this way, his gold fever never ceasing, always hoping to fill his pockets with it once more.

Several miles from here there is a certain Jack, the son of an American and an Indian woman, who inherited all the unenviable characteristics of a savage from his mother without acquiring any qualities of a white man from his father. This Jack lives on his government plot; he lives by gun alone, lives filthily, lazily, and prizes whiskey and tobacco. Sometimes Jack needs money he doesn't have, for whiskey and taxes. Then Jack goes to Markell and Markell gives it to him. And so it went for several years until the debt and interest became so large that, one fine morning, poor Jack had to set off to Placerville and turn his farm over to Markell. This happened during the time we were staying in the mountains. Both of them returned very drunk and both pleased. I don't know why Jack was happy, probably in part from natural *joie de vivre* freshened by the influence of whiskey. Markell had a more concrete reason. On Jack's farm, where the former owner now stays as a watchman, there is excellent land, excellent forest and, most importantly, a gold mine that Markell had been eyeing voraciously for a long time.

Because he doesn't have capital for gold-producing enterprises, old Markell leads a contemplative life. Either he sits at home on the porch smoking a short little pipe and looks at these mountains filled with gold, or he reads the newspaper; when there is no newspaper, he reads an old chemistry textbook. In general he is not without some education, a bit of a philosopher, and his natural wit enables him to feel at home in any sphere. It is very pleasant to talk with him, especially because he is not averse to talking and he won't say anything without weighing it or thinking it over first.

A mile or two from Markell and Cook lives their nearest neighbor, also an old bachelor and a settler on a government plot. His little farm is even less developed and more neglected than Markell's farm. All you can see there is a bad, untended garden, in the middle of which stands a dilapidated shack that looks more like a pigpen. Rain, snow, sun, and wind have free access through the huge cracks in the rotting walls and roof. The inside is dirty and empty. How and where this Diogenes sleeps, he alone knows, because neither a bed nor any other sort of furniture is to be seen. He is of some sort of Irish extraction. He lives on the farm only during the summer; in winter he leaves for lower parts; I don't know how well or by what means he lives there. Here in the summer he has company and gives shelter to some suspicious-looking young people who drive their cattle up for summer pasture. The whole lot of them produce meat, supplying the entire region with it. Because these alien cattle strip grazing land, and also because this group takes advantage of the absence of control and kills other peoples' cows for the meat, they are hardly regarded with good will by Golden, Markell, and other settled farmers.

On this side of the deep ravine, in the depths of which rumbles the marvelous Slab Creek with its multitude of picturesque waterfalls and pools full of trout, with its cool freshness

Courtesy of the El Dorado County Historical Museum

Mosquito Bridge over the American River, ca. 1891

and shadowy, wild, infrequently crossed banks, a new mountain looms up in a steep wall completely overgrown with beautiful timber. There on an elevated plateau there is still much free land. Several plots have already been taken by young people from neighboring towns. Most of them are not honest settlers, but merely agents of a rich capitalist company attempting to grab the forest in its hands. Huge tracts already belong to it. The system by which it is seized is very simple. Once they have found several dozen unscrupulous agents who haven't lost their rights to government land, they send them to the land bureau in Placerville. Exercising their right, they choose the best forest plots, for appearance's sake construct lean-tos on them, and, having satisfied the legal formalities, resell the land to the company as soon as they receive the right to dispose of it. Several take plots at their own risk, and once the allotted time has elapsed they sell the timber to the same company and keep the land for further speculation.

The result: Very soon, axes will ring through these virgin forests, locomotives will whistle, and the forests' ruin will begin. And then the dried-up streams and countryside will turn into a lifeless desert something like the one that now stretches between the Sierra Nevada and the Rocky Mountains. American individualistic ways of doing things are far from posing a serious obstacle to this course of events. The Americans will wake up to it only when it's too late.

Cranks, Princes, and Land-grabbers

Part II

1

The Making of a Revolutionary in Exile

Even for late-19th-century San Francisco, where between 1887 and 1892 Nicholas Russel practiced medicine (eye, ear, nose, and throat) from an office on California Street and then in the Phelan Building, the author of "Around California" was a man with an unusual biography.

The circumstances of Russel's birth and youth seem to have conspired to produce a polyglot and cosmopolitan. He was born Nikolai Konstantinovich Sudzilovskii on December 3, 1850, into a Russified family of Polish gentry origin in what was then western Russia, had been (until 1772) part of Poland, and is

now in the Byelorussian Republic of the USSR. His father, who had a legal education, served in the Russian judicial administration of Mogilev province and was registered as a nobleman of that province.

The younger Sudzilovskii, who graduated from the *Gymnasium* in Mogilev, matriculated in law in 1868 at the university in the Russian capital of St. Petersburg before transferring in 1869 to the university in Kiev (today the capital of the Ukrainian Republic), where he switched to medicine. After finishing four years, he set aside his studies in favor of revolutionary politics, which led in 1875 to his fleeing the country to avoid arrest. He never returned to Russia. He completed his medical education in 1876 at the University of Bucharest, in Romania. In 1877, still in Bucharest, Sudzilovskii officially changed his name to Russel, and his doctoral thesis, a treatise on antiseptic methods in surgery, was published in Romanian under that name.[1] He went by the name Russel for the rest of his life.

Sudzilovskii changed his name in 1877 to avoid the likelihood of arrest and deportation by the Russian military authorities, who were about to occupy Romania in the Russo-Turkish War (1877–78). The choice of the name "Russel" was ingenious: It was suitable for the American background its bearer fabricated for himself at this time; yet it testified, for those in the know, to his real origins: "Russel" in Romanian means "Russian."

Although various biographers have claimed Polish, Byelorussian, and even Ukrainian nationality for him, Sudzilovskii/Russel thought of himself as a *Russian*: The language of instruction throughout his education before emigration was Russian; Russian appears to have been the only Slavic language in which he wrote, not only for publication, but even in correspondence with members of his immediate family; and he invariably referred to himself as a Russian in his writings.[2]

Russel's choice of an American background and an American-sounding name in 1877 was not accidental.

The two decades of the 1860s and 1870s, those straddled by Russel's Russian university years, were a time of extraordinary, unprecedented ideological and political ferment among the educated youth of the Russian Empire. Following Russia's humiliating defeat in the Crimean War (1854–56) at the hands of the industrializing powers England and France, the autocratic regime of the new Emperor, Alexander II, embarked on a course of *perestroika* designed to overcome backwardness and restore Russia to eminence, if not pre-eminence, among the great powers.

The "Great Reforms" of those years, whose centerpiece and *sine qua non* was the abolition of serfdom (1861), upset the foundations of the traditional order of things and introduced into Russian life the *principles*, at least, of modern jurisprudence, equality before the law and equality of opportunity, freedom of speech and press, and even public participation in governance. An important part of the modernizing strategy was an expansion of education in general, and of university education in particular: For the first time, building on foundations laid earlier in the century, the student population of the half-dozen universities in the principal cities of the empire reached proportions necessary to sustain—together with recent graduates, drop-outs, would-be students, upper-form *Gymnasium* pupils, and hangers-on of both sexes (only men could officially enroll in Russian universities)—a kind of student subculture. The average university student body in 1880 was about 1,000; the subculture in any university town was probably at least two or three times that size.

In *practice*—for lack of capital, infrastructure, and training, and because the autocrat had no intention of limiting his authority as a goal of his reforms—things remained afterward very much they way they had been before: The peasants, who constituted 85 percent of the population, remained mired in their illiterate and traditional ways and, once the dust of reform had settled, seemed to many observers to be actually worse off than before; society as a whole remained highly stratified. The gap between privileged Russia, educated in the European style, and the masses was, if anything, growing; discussion of "rights" was to a large extent restricted to the pages of academic treatises; the autocracy remained intact.

Thus, in a stroke, Russia experienced the growth to sociologically significant proportions of a body of idealistic, educated youth, drawn largely from the sons and daughters of the nobility, but leavened by a strong admixture of value- and style-setting commoners; great expectations engendered by the politics of *perestroika*, absolute-monarchy style; and the failure of these expectations in the realization of the reforms. The coalescence of these circumstances transformed this youth culture, almost as a whole, into a counterculture, an intelligentsia, devoted to seeking a radical transformation of Russian reality. This was the beginning of the movement that eventually led to the Bolshevik Revolution of 1917 and the world's first socialist state.

The years extending from the late 1860s through the entire decade of the 1870s are known in the history of the Russian revolutionary movement as the epoch of revolutionary populism. In a still pre-industrial society, the movement's designated beneficiary, toward which the privileged youth felt indebted,—even guilty—was, of course, the peasantry. This group was endowed in the minds of the revolting youth with natural socialist propensities (reflected in the communal practices, such as periodic land redistribution, that were still widely practiced by peasant villages), hostility toward centralized political authority, and a preference for loose federal arrangements bordering on anarchy. The children of Russia's elite were moved by the vision of an agrarian utopia.

The populist era began with the formation, in the late 1860s and early 1870s, of underground circles, mostly nothing more than study groups for political consciousness-raising—the reading and discussion of radical political and social theories, the history of the European labor movement, and last but far from least, the writings of Marx. An illegal translation of *The Communist Manifesto* was available as early as 1863, and the first volume of *Das Kapital* was published in Russian translation in 1869—legally! It passed the censors as a dull academic treatise. Under the impact of this literature, even the first steps of the Russian government towards economic development in the form of railroadization were greeted with hostility by the populists: Such steps threatened to usher in the horrors of capitalist exploitation and political rule by the bourgeoisie, which would only make realization of the agrarian utopia that much more difficult.

But the radical youths made no significant headway among the peasants with their alien ways and ideas, and being unorganized and naively open about their purposes, they were sitting ducks for arrest by the aroused police. Veterans of the movement who managed to avoid detention gradually became involved in terrorist activities against the government. By the late 1870s the terrorists had concentrated their attack on the person of the tsar, and, after several failed attempts, succeeded in assassinating Alexander II on March 1, 1881. The result of this campaign was the opposite of that intended: The new tsar, Alexander III, embarked on a course of repression and reaction that prolonged the life of autocracy.

Nikolai Sudzilovskii was in many ways a typical representative of the revolutionary-populist generation of the Russian intelligentsia; instead of being arrested and sent to Siberian exile or entering the terrorist movement in the second half of the 1870s, he fled abroad. In his *Gymnasium* days in the mid-1860s he had been a proper "nihilist"—a believer in the power of science and reason to improve humanity's lot, a worshipper of the natural sciences, especially chemistry. He enrolled in the law faculty at Petersburg University, probably out of respect for his father; but forced to leave at the end of his first year as a result of involvement in a student protest movement over disciplinary issues, he chose to transfer to medicine. Here he could pursue both his interest in science and social commitment.

As a medical student in Kiev, Sudzilovskii immediately got involved in the populist movement. By 1871, he had advanced from "literary" or self-enlightenment pursuits to the conviction that the future of mankind lay in anarcho-communism, the abolition of private property and the state. With his friends, he began to lay plans for creating a "commune" that would serve as a model of the future order for others.

This was the origin of the "American circle," formed among medical students in 1871. Its central idea, of which Sudzilovskii appears to have been the main proponent, was to emigrate to "free America" and establish a model commune there.

Thoughts naturally turned to the New World, where there already existed a considerable tradition of utopian-communal experiments, on both religious and secular foundations, from the Shakers and the Mormons to the Oneida Community and Robert Owen's New Harmony.[3]

Apparently the only thing that prevented emigration en masse to the United States was lack of funds. Sudzilovskii's group finally collected some money, mainly from a cash dowry accessed through a fictitious marriage between a member of the group and a sympathetic young noblewoman. The cash was deposited in a Parisian bank with a New York branch, and in late 1872 and early 1873 two groups of three each set out for America.[4] The first of these, consisting of Grigorii Machtet, Ivan Rechitskii, and A. Roman'ko-Romanovskii, were sent off as a scouting party to "choose the place for the new colony." By December 1872 they had made it as far as Kansas. There Romanovskii was accidentally shot and killed by Rechitskii, and the two survivors split up.[5] Apparently disenchanted with their mission and out of funds (with Rechitskii, to boot, suffering psychologically from the fatal accident), both soon returned to Russia. Machtet went on to became a fairly popular writer (scenes from American life were one of his staples) and later endured Siberian exile.[6] Rechitskii participated in the revolutionary activities of 1874, was arrested in the town of Nikolaevsk (Samara province), and shot himself either during a preliminary search of his quarters by agents of the Third Section, the political police, or on the way to prison. (The former seems more plausible: How could he have had access to a firearm on the way to prison?)

The second group, consisting of Sudzilovskii and two comrades, set out for America in the spring of 1873. But they got no further than Zurich, where they were supposed to wait for word from Kansas and make financial arrangements for the trip. Here they found a large and thoroughly radicalized Russian colony that included some political exiles but was mostly made up of students, chiefly young noblewomen pursuing the higher education they had been denied in Russia. According to Sudzilovskii's later recollection, they found that the idea of setting up communes in America was already losing popularity in the Zurich colony in favor of plans for carrying the revolution to the people at home.[7] This was the build-up to revolutionary actions that were perhaps given a decisive impulse by the return home to Russia of most of the Zurich women students at the end of 1873, following an ultimatum by the Russian government.

In Zurich, Sudzilovskii and his comrades came to identify themselves with the revolutionary anarchism espoused by Mikhail Bakunin. In the meantime they heard of the Kansas tragedy and learned that the appropriated dowry they had been counting on for their American adventure had disappeared in a bankruptcy. They abandoned the idea of traveling to the United States.

Sudzilovskii soon returned to Kiev, where he resumed his studies. But he quickly abandoned school for the "Kiev

Commune," a conspiratorial living experiment that became a kind of clearing house and training center for revolutionary youth. Sudzilovskii himself worked as a village paramedic, then spent several months on the move eluding the police, and finally fled abroad at the beginning of 1875. It was "either east to Siberian exile or west of Russia as refugees," and he took the latter. He was 25 years old.

Sudzilovskii spent the first nine months of his exile in western Europe, first in London and then in Geneva, working in hospitals, becoming acquainted with the Russian revolutionary expatriates and the leading figures of European socialism (Marx and Engels) and writing for the radical emigré press. His principal biographer also has him making a lightning trip to New York in April–May 1875 for purposes of obtaining dynamite for terrorist acts in Russia. Another account even has him acquiring U.S. citizenship under the name "John Russel" on this trip. The last assertion, at least, is clearly false: Sudzilovskii himself testifies that he applied for American citizenship only during his stay in San Francisco, after having a request to return to Russia under amnesty denied him.[8]

In any event, in the autumn of 1875 Sudzilovskii and his bride-to-be (to whom he had proposed already in Russia) moved to Bucharest, where he finished his medical schooling in 1876. For the next five years he lived in Bucharest and Jassy, practicing medicine under the name of Dr. Russel, doing medical research, and engaging in radical-socialist politics and journalism. In 1881, he was expelled from Romania for organizing a demonstration celebrating the tenth anniversary of the Paris Commune and the assassination of Tsar Alexander II. Put on a boat for Constantinople, where they were to have been turned over to the Russian authorities, Sudzilovskii a.k.a. Russel, his wife, and their two small girls managed to elude the authorities upon docking in Turkey.

There followed some seven years of more-or-less transient

existence, temporary employment, and radical activity in western Europe and the Balkans; a good part of this time was spent in Bulgaria (eastern Rumelia before the unification of Bulgaria in 1885). Here Russel and his wife parted. She returned with their daughters to her gentry family in Chernigov province, Russia, in 1883. Russel obtained a legal divorce and then, before leaving for America, married one of the former female Russian students in Zurich.[9]

While in Rumelia, Russel had opposed the prospective unification of Bulgaria under Prince Battenberg as likely to lead to a reactionary order under Austrian domination. A typical *narodnik* (revolutionary populist) of the 1870s, he dreamed of turning Bulgaria's agrarian backwardness and relative lack of social differentiation into an asset—a foundation for a revolutionary leap directly into socialism.[10] He appears to have taken an active part in the preparation of the "September Revolution" (1885) that led, all the same, to the unification of Bulgaria.

In any event, once the unification became reality, Russel found himself at odds with the new regime and the Russian consulate, as well as with his former allies in the Bulgarian independence movement. Accusations of collaboration with the Russian secret police flourished, and Russel found it impossible to stay on. His Bulgarian experience may have revived his dream of finding in America "freer and more favorable soil" for realizing his internationalist, collectivist ideas.[11] It may also be that, having been run out of—or put on the wanted list in—most of the states of eastern and southeastern Europe and unlikely to find suitable employment in western Europe with a Romanian medical degree, his European options were simply exhausted. Russel arrived in New York in August 1887, and by October was in San Francisco.

The Bishop and the Schoolboys

We don't know why Russel chose to settle in California. Perhaps the stories of Bret Harte he had read in his youth had something to do with it. Or it may be that he followed his younger brother to San Francisco.

The Russian consular records in San Francisco show that Emil Konstantinovich Sudzilovskii obtained a passport for foreign travel in January 1887 and came to San Francisco.[1] He was still in town in June 1889 to attend a meeting of the parishioners of St. Nicholas Russian Orthodox Church, where a petition to the Holy Synod in St. Petersburg demanding the

recall of the Orthodox Bishop Vladimir was signed by him and 24 others, including his older brother. He figures subsequently in the Bishop's letter of anathema against Russel, dated January 21, 1890, where his testimony is cited in support of the Bishop's allegations of bigamy and flight from justice. After that, Emil drops out of our sight entirely.[2]

Russel, it can be seen, did not spend his time in San Francisco in seclusion from public affairs. That he would get into a row with the Church was only to be expected: In the absence of a revolutionary movement or even a decent national liberation struggle, what better outlet for the radical energies of that enemy of the Russian autocracy and establishment religion than corruption in the Orthodox Church—the state church, no less, whose administration was in fact a branch of the Russian government, headed at this time by the most notoriously reactionary figure in Petersburg, the Procurator of the Holy Synod, K.P. Pobedonostsev.[3] And Bishop Vladimir offered Russel scandal, as it were, on a plate.

A Russian Orthodox diocese for North America[4] had been established in 1840. Its see was located in Sitka, Alaska. Shortly after the sale of Alaska to the United States in 1867, the see was moved to San Francisco, ostensibly for purposes of better communication with the mother church and for better propagation of the faith throughout North America (critics maintained, however, that the move was for the greater comfort of the bishops). Most of the parishes and faithful, the latter numbering 8,000–10,000 in the 1880s, were located in Alaska: San Francisco had a miniscule Orthodox population of Russians, Greeks, Serbs and assorted other "Slavonians," or Orthodox South Slavs.

The bishopric was plagued by scandal almost from the moment of its arrival in San Francisco. Ioann Mitropol'skii, the first Bishop of Alaska and the Aleutians to take up residence in San Francisco, was recalled after a few years in an odor of scandal involving a sexual appetite for schoolgirls and prostitutes.

Ioann's brother Nikita, also a monk, remained in Alaska but gained such notoriety throughout the diocese for drunkenness, licentiousness, and intrigue that in 1886 the consul-general in San Francisco felt compelled to write a letter to Procurator Pobedonostsev in Petersburg begging him to recall Nikita to Russia for the sake of the Church's and the country's reputation.[5]

Ioann's temporary replacement, the archpriest Kedrolivanskii, soon became the object of rivalrous attacks by another priest assigned to the diocese.[6] At one a.m. on June 10, 1880, Kedrolivanskii was found near the corner of California and Webb Streets "in a dying condition . . . , terribly sandbagged." He expired the next day in hospital. His rival, suspected of having had him waylaid, was (according to the *San Francisco Examiner*) immediately recalled to Russia and confined to a monastery; the San Francisco police dropped the case.

After a brief interlude, a successor who had previously served as a priest in Japan arrived and proceeded, according to custom, to conduct an audit of the diocesan books. According to the *Examiner,* he discovered much dishonesty among church officials in the diocese, but could not bring himself to denounce them to the Synod. Moreover, he appears to have continued Ioann's practice of filling the parishes in his diocese with priests who were "altogether lacking in education and for the most part of unsober comportment." In 1882, on a trip to Alaska, the new bishop drowned. There were rumors of murder, but the consensus in the Russian community seems to have been that it was a suicide, perhaps brought on by despondency over church affairs.

A respectable interlude followed for the next several years, during which the diocese was administered by an archpriest of apparently unimpeachable honesty. Then came Bishop Vladimir, who arrived in San Francisco in April 1888, some seven months after Dr. Russel. The trouble began almost as soon as the train bearing Vladimir and his large entourage pulled into the station.

He immediately set about drastically abbreviating the salaries of some church employees, firing others and replacing them with people from his retinue, eliminating various pensions, and cutting back on the upkeep of the fifteen to twenty Eskimo and Indian boys who had been brought from Alaska to a Church-run seminary for training as teachers of their people. A dispute arose with some parishioners over the Bishop's refusal to have the Church take over an Orthodox cemetery protected by the local "Greek-Russian-Slavonic Benevolent Society." At the same time, he commenced major renovation and expansion projects around the episcopal residence at 1713–15 Powell Street.[7] In this way, Vladimir began to accumulate enemies in the small Russian colony.

A year passed without major incident. Then, in the early morning of May 21, 1889, the Russian church burned down. Rumors, accusations, and counter-accusations flew fast and furious. Some of the Bishop's enemies suspected him of setting

Bishop Vladimir

the fire in order to collect the insurance and engage in even more grandiose building projects. Others blamed it on his corner-cutting: The caretaker, whose job it was to look after the candles and censers used in the church, had been fired. One of the Bishop's supporters responded with intimations that embezzlers or other malefactors were to blame: They wanted to destroy incriminating records or disputed real-estate titles held in the Church, or maybe the Bishop himself. The Bishop told the newspapers it was probably just hoodlums after gold and silver plate, but he also intimated that the source of the Church's troubles in general were "outcasts, Nihilists, of whom there are a number in this city."[8]

At a June 1 meeting of the Greek-Russian-Slavonic Benevolent Society, a petition was drawn up, signed by most of the thirty-odd persons attending, and sent to Pobedonostsev in Petersburg. The petition laid out a bill of eleven particulars against Bishop Vladimir, ranging from his having replaced Church Slavonic in church services with fractured English ("which neither we nor the Americans can understand . . . , which not only disturbs our prayerful mood but makes the Americans laugh") to mismanagement of the church budget, allegedly resulting in the impoverishment of the staff, neglect of charitable works, and the church fire. The eleventh point read:

"In view of his cruel, unchristian behavior toward the school pupils, clergymen, and parishioners, as well as his inability to carry out the responsibilities of his elevated post, Bishop Vladimir should be recalled from our diocese and replaced by another person."

The irate parishioners also sent a statement to Vladimir himself, asking him to stop further construction work pending a ruling from the Holy Synod and castigating him for his offensive characterization of the Russian colony in San Francisco in his interview with newspaper reporters (that is, the remark about "outcasts and Nihilists"). The chairman of the meeting, author of both the covering letter to Pobedonostsev and the exhortation to Vladimir, was none other than the Vice-President of the Greek-Russian-Slavonic Benevolent Society and most prominent Nihilist in town, Dr. Nicholas Russel.[9]

Vladimir immediately responded with a letter to Russel that was an artful mixture of patient explanation and threat. First, the explanations: The construction projects conformed to the requirements of an episcopal residence and were financed directly by the Synod, not by parish funds; many parishioners do not understand Slavonic; the petitioners' appeals directly to the Synod were illegal; the reporters had distorted his words, and so on. Then, the threats: "You are an enemy of God by conviction. To avoid temptation, I forbid you entrance into the episcopal house and church. If you do not desist from sedition and repent, you will be publicly anathematized in accordance with the 28th apostolic rule."[10]

It must have been around this time that Russel began inquiring into the rumors he had been hearing since Vladimir's arrival in town about the Bishop's unusual relationship with several members of a group of young boys, none of them over 14 years of age, that he had brought with him from Russia and installed in the Church's school. All of them—with the exception of one William Allen, an English boy who had joined the Bishop's entourage in Petersburg—were Russians who Vladimir had persuaded (directly or via their parents) to come to the New World with the Bishop to obtain an education and a career in the Church.

It was in fact from a parent of two of the boys, a patient of Russel's named Martysh, that the doctor first got confirmation of rumors that the Bishop was having sexual relations with some of the boys. According to Martysh's unedifying story, Vladimir had taken a liking to the boys at the seminary in Chelm (in Russian Poland), where they were pupils and he the director before his transfer to San Francisco. When he was appointed to the American post, he was able to keep the two boys with him only by bringing the whole family to California and promising an Alaskan parish to the father as soon as he had gotten through the preliminary offices. In San Francisco the father, on the one hand, apparently became fully aware of the nature of the relations between the Bishop and the boys, which he had only suspected at home, and Vladimir, on the other hand, showed no sign of honoring his promise. Martysh at this point proceeded to blackmail the Bishop by threatening to denounce his "crime against nature," sodomy, to Pobedonostsev. The affair came just short of that before Vladimir yielded and, in writing, promised Martysh a choice parish in Alaska.[11]

The next person to try blackmail on the Bishop was one of the other boys, Alexander Bobovsky. In September 1889, Bobovsky left the school and went to a lawyer to recover some money and goods allegedly promised by the Bishop in a contract signed with Bobovsky before they left Russia. In the round of demands and disclaimers that followed between the lawyer, Edward Myers, and the Bishop, Myers proceeded from vague warnings of "unpleasantness" to the revelation that his client was accusing Vladimir of "crimes against morality of the most loathsome kind." This was after the Bishop had tried to bypass the lawyer and settle with Bobovsky through the intermediary of the Russian vice-consul. Whether a settlement was ever reached is not known. Bobovsky, like several of the other boys involved in the scandal, returned to Russia in the spring of 1891, apparently with money provided by Pobedonostsev through the Russian consulate.[12]

Russel went on collecting evidence about the Bishop and the schoolboys until he had at least six more testimonies, several of them notarized. At some point he also hired a private detective to put a tail on Vladimir.

The nature of these goings-on soon became known in the consulate and in the Orthodox community in San Francisco.[13]

The Bishop decided to act against Russel. First he convened a Consistory (church court) and had it issue a summons to Russel on December 12, 1889, to appear before it at Diocesan headquarters on December 19 on charges of using a false name, bigamy, slander, and "arousing Orthodox parishioners against the Diocesan administration." Russel replied with a brief letter denying both the accusations and the Consistory's jurisdiction in the United States. A December 24 letter from the Bishop threatened him with anathema should he fail to appear before the Church administration on January 3, 1990.

At this point Russel went to a lawyer, E.L. Campbell, while the Bishop set about drafting his letter of excommunication. The acting Russian consul, Gustav Niebaum, on learning that Russel was contemplating legal action against the Church, tried to defuse the scandal by instructing the consulate's Montgomery Street lawyer, Horace G. Platt, to contact Campbell to find out what action was being contemplated and what the likely consequences for the Church and the Bishop would be.[14]

Platt reported a week later that he had been to see Campbell ("a lawyer of very good standing, [who] would not engage in any blackmailing affair"), who claimed that his client had a good case against the Bishop; that he had been slandered by the Bishop, and his practice as physician among Church parishioners almost ruined by the Bishop's action; and that unless the Bishop was recalled immediately and Russel were paid $50,000 for injury to his practice, he would bring criminal charges against the Bishop. Russel, Platt reported, "is intensely bitter in this matter, and seems determined to be revenged upon the Bishop at any cost."

Platt tried to get Russel to drop the case by arguing that the Bishop had no money and that going to court would broadcast the as yet little-known charges against Russel, but this did no good. Russel was determined to bring a civil action against the Bishop for slander and seek a judgment for damages to his reputation. He also intended to have the Bishop arrested for libel—the accusations of the Consistory letter—and get a conviction for that crime. Platt was somewhat skeptical about the likelihood of a conviction in this case, but allowed that the Bishop had put himself in "a very dangerous position."

"The worst part of the whole matter, however," Platt continued, "is the scandal that would be created by [Russel's] instituting criminal proceedings against the Bishop for his alleged illicit intercourse with some of the boys in the school." Campbell claimed to have proof (obviously provided by Russel) that the Bishop "has been guilty of the 'crime against nature' with several of these little boys." Platt allowed that the charges would be difficult to prove, "unless the boys could be induced to testify against themselves," but the very accusation "would scandalize the entire community."

Platt concluded: "After due deliberation, I think the matter is in a very precarious condition. The Bishop has been very unwise, and it will require the very strongest efforts to pull him through, if even that much can be done. I would advise that you call the attention of your government very earnestly to this matter."[15]

But by this time, the Bishop had already pronounced anathema on Russel in church. And on January 21 he put his signature to a formal writ of excommunication, replete with the familiar charges and references to various Church Councils and Apostolic Rules,[16] and sent it to Russel.[17]

Back in Petersburg, Pobedonostsev, having seen Platt's message, realized that *raison d'état* dictated that he recall Vladimir and get the boys out of the country. Russel received a telegram at his 1529 California Street address directly from Pobedonostsev, dated February 18: "Letter received—Answer post—bishop recalled—what want you more process nuisance for all. Pobedonostseff." The Western Union copy of the telegram was later examined and verified by the *Examiner* reporter who published it.[18] Russel also provided the papers with what he claimed was the text of a telegram sent by the Holy Synod to the consul-general: "Russel's anathema found null and void by the Holy Synod. Bishop recalled. You may publish that in the local papers. Pobedonostzeff." It was not, however, published by either the consulate or the Church; it was printed only a year later from copy provided by Russel.[19]

At the later date, as well, Russel provided the newspapers a letter he alleged Pobedonostsev had sent to the Archimandrite Inokentii on June 16, 1890, inquiring after Pobedonostsev's earlier order to Inokentii to take over the episcopal church and all Church properties from Vladimir, whom he thought to be psychologically unbalanced. Vladimir, wrote the Procurator, should be persuaded to return to Russia at the earliest opportunity. (It appears that at the time the scandal broke Inokentii was in North America on a missionary tour.)[20]

But the Bishop did not leave in three weeks, or in three months. He stayed on, fast in his denial of the recall, until November 1891, when he departed suddenly. In his interview with a *Chronicle* reporter on August 28, 1891, Vladimir said that Inokentii had returned to Petersburg in November 1890, "perfectly satisfied with my administration."[21] The Bishop also refused (at least for a time) the services of Horace Platt, who had been engaged by the consulate on orders from Petersburg to defend him in the case brought by Russel. Vladimir had no use for Niebaum's help.[22]

The consular records leave no doubt that the Bishop had indeed been recalled to Petersburg by the Holy Synod in early 1890. How was he able to ignore orders from Church and State in this fashion? The answer seems to be that they had no effective instruments of control over this bishopric on foreign soil. They could not cut off Vladimir's source of funds because the Church's property, in San Francisco at least, belonged to the Bishop himself in the eyes of U.S. law.[23]

Around California in 1891

Once it became clear that Vladimir was not about to leave town, Russel and his lawyer, Campbell, tried to get the District Attorney, a man named Page, to bring an indictment against the Bishop on the morals charge, but Page only turned the case over to Judge Joachimsen's police court, where it languished. In August 1890, one Nicholas Fedoroff took up the mission and brought before the grand jury the written testimonies of several of Vladimir's alleged juvenile victims: Allen, Kucheriavyi, and Vanna. But Horace Platt (according to the anti-Vladimir party) got to the mayor, who had Page present the affair to the jury as blackmail. None of the boys were called to testify; the Bishop, Russel, and Niebaum were. The Bishop (still according to the anti-Vladimir group's version of these events) was let off by the grand jury with these approximate words: "We release you not because we have found you innocent, but out of respect for the Church whose head you are."[24]

The Bishop was undaunted. He set about collecting information on Russel, and at the turn of the new year, 1891, he sent Russel an "exhortation" calling on him to repent and "get quietly out of town," lest things go bad for him. To show Russel what was in store for him, Vladimir offered a list of Russel's crimes on which he claimed to have evidence: These included details about Russel-Sudzilovskii's flights from justice and participation in a prison break-out, all prior to his final flight from Russia in 1875; the attempted murder of E.L. Kochetov (L'vov), a correspondent for a conservative Russian newspaper, in Bulgaria; cruelty to his (Russel's) own wife and children in Turkey; and a few other items. To top it all off the Bishop included a photograph of Russel's first wife—which she had sent, he wrote, "as a reminder of his responsibility to have but one wife and to help with his children's education." On the right-hand margin were the words: "This is the mother of your children, who advises you to come to your senses before it is too late." And on the left: "If your crimes are revealed in court, you won't receive American citizenship."[25]

Russel answered the Bishop with a one-sentence letter, addressed "To Vladimir, the Alaskan and Aleutian Sodomist," which was a virtuosity of untranslatable Russian maternal cursing. It ended with the warning that if the Bishop did not stop bothering him with his execrable letters, Russel would pay him a visit, not to make peace, but to castrate him.[26] In the letter accompanying the copies of this "correspondence" that he sent to the consulate, Russel begged Niebaum's pardon for the language of his letter to Vladimir: It was the tone Vladimir's missive merited; it was either that or a thrashing, which didn't seem wise insofar as he, Russel, had a civil suit pending against the Bishop. For the same reason, he wrote, he would not file a criminal charge of blackmail against the Bishop. Moreover, it was better to be a defendant in a criminal case. Let the Bishop bring charges against him: He would welcome the chance to have a Russian political trial in an American court, which is what the Bishop's case would amount to. It would be an opportunity to expose the cruelty and absurdity of the Russian regime's political persecutions—as well as the highly unenviable role of Vladimir in them, compromising as they were for the Church—not to mention an opportunity to answer the unfounded accusations about Russel's marital status and family relations. Here, it seems, Russel summed up the essential motives of his campaign against the Bishop.

Niebaum returned Russel's "correspondence" with the Bishop along with the comment that it was no concern of the consulate. This, however, did not prevent Niebaum from having two sets of copies made: One went in the consular file; the other he sent to the Washington mission. "I must confess," he wrote to the Russian ambassador in Washington, K.V. Struve, in a covering letter, "that I am getting heartily sick of this disgustingly nasty mess, and only wish that someone would be appointed soon to relieve me. I have tried my best to keep peace in the family and so far it has been tolerable successful, but am afraid the whole business will break out again with renewed vigor."[27]

Niebaum's apprehensions were soon justified. In early May, a disgruntled former priest in the Bishop's church by the name of Joseph Levin ("an apostate Jew" the Bishop described him for the press), one of those whose salaries had been cut in half, blew the whistle on the treatment of the children in the church school to the local Society for the Prevention of Cruelty to Children. In a letter to the SPCC dated May 16, Levin's lawyer, Edward Myers, said he had that very day visited the school at 1713 Powell Street, where he had discovered "about a dozen boys from 6 to 14 years of age, who one and all complained to me that they were confined there without sufficient food, and whose physical appearance bore ample testimony to the fact that they were strangers to soap and water and decent or sufficient clothing."[28]

The SPCC alerted the police, who sent an officer, George Comstock, to the school in the company of Secretary Charles Holbrook of the SPCC. There they found fourteen boys, none over 14 years of age, "huddled together in a small dormitory, the filth of which was frightful and from which the odors that arose were sickening. The boys reported they were beaten, starved, and otherwise ill-treated." The policeman issued a warning, then returned a few days later, found no changes, and arrested E.P. Alexine, the superintendent of the school, and his assistant Paul Ligda. Twelve or fourteen boys, depending on the account, were removed from the school to City Prison, and thence to the Youth's Directory on Howard Street, near 17th, where they were installed as wards of the city.

There is some uncertainty about the identity of these boys. In some newspaper accounts they are described as Eskimos or Indians from Alaska, or "Esquimaux, Indian, and half-breed boys." Ex-father Levin is quoted in the *Daily Report* for June 11 as saying: "These boys are all Esquimaux-Indians." Three of them, Nicholas Mercurieff (Merkul'ev) (age 11), George Kachigin (Grigorii Kochergin), and Nicholas King (age 12½), were among the boys who had testified to being sexually abused by the Bishop.[29] All three may have been the children of Eskimo or Indian mothers and white fathers, in the first two cases evidently Russians. The names of the boys who are known to have come from Russia with the Bishop and allegedly had sexual relations with him—the Martysh boys, Bobovsky, and Allen—are not among them. Evidently they had all been sent back to Russia before the raid on the school.

For some weeks the story was big news, illustrated with sketches of the principals and scenes from "the dungeon on Powell Street." By June 15, the news had reached Pobedonostsev. He cabled Niebaum: "Some new scandal reported. Please inform me."

The papers linked the arrest of Alexine and Ligda to the history of troubles surrounding the Bishop and the Church, but they did not go so far as to link the "Alexine case" to the morals charges on which the Bishop's enemies had been trying to get him arrested for over a year. Lawyer Platt, of course, saw the connection: On June 17, he prepared a damage report for Niebaum at the consulate in which he described the affair as "only another effort on the part of certain parties to bring scandal upon the Bishop. I think that these efforts will continue as long as he is here. Having failed to accomplish anything in their past efforts against the Bishop, they have been more successful in this last movement." Nevertheless, he surmised, the present case could not affect Church property, as it involved only personal charges against Alexine and Ligda, who were in charge of the school during the Bishop's absence, and it seemed unlikely the charges of cruelty brought against them could be proved.

Platt may have been more right than he knew in his characterization of this new battle in the campaign against the Bishop as "more successful": Russel's papers contain excerpts from various Petersburg newspapers for August–September 1891, indicating that the basic decision to transfer Vladimir (as it turned out, to the see of Voronezh in central Russia) and to appoint Nicholas of Kherson in his place was made in the Synod in June.[30] But it would take time for the wheels of bureaucracy to grind through the various Church and government instances. The Bishop, if he knew about this process, did not let on about it for the time being. Nor did the consulate.

When Vladimir returned to town from his Alaska tour in late August, he gave an interview to the *Chronicle* (August 27; issue of August 28) in which he vigorously asserted that all the accusations against him personally and the Church in general were lies, the doings of "fugitive Russians, nihilists fleeing from punishment, and fugitive Russian Jews. Their attacks, though ostensibly directed against me personally, are really prompted by a desire to injure the State and the Church." Vladimir was now denying that he had ever been recalled at all (for whatever purpose), and he was seconded in this by the newly appointed consul-general, V.A. Artsimovich. Artsimovich also told the reporter that "he was convinced that all the atrocious charges made against the Bishop were groundless. "We may send the Bishop away," he allowed, because of the persistence of the charges (Artsimovich must have known about the transfer process that was underway in Petersburg before he left there) but, he added in seeming contradiction, "we have no right to do so, and if he wishes to remain it is his privilege."

These utterances, said the *Chronicle*'s story of the next day (August 29), "considerably excited that part of the Russian population here opposed to [the Bishop's] regime and have called out certain documents." It was at this point that Russel trotted out for the newspapers the Pobedonostsev telegrams of February and March 1890 concerning the Bishop's recall; excerpts of the alleged letter of Pobedonostsev to Inokentii also appeared in the press at this time.

The Bishop immediately declared all these documents forgeries: "They have been made out of whole cloth and are the forgeries of a perverted man, Dr. Russel himself." And Artsimovich again seconded the Bishop: "I am unable to find in the papers of my predecessor," he was quoted as saying, "any cablegram announcing Vladimir's recall, and I certainly have received no such notification." Artsimovich may have been telling the literal truth—there may have been no such telegrams in his files—but there was plenty of evidence about Vladimir's recall in his predecessor's correspondence. It seems reasonably clear that Artsimovich had been instructed before leaving Petersburg to defend the Bishop against the "nihilists."

Russel's reply to Vladimir's accusation of forgery was to swear out a warrant in Judge Joachimsen's court on September 7 for the arrest of Vladimir on charges of "libel of forgery" (the Bishop's other libelous charges—bigamy and "nihilism"—were described as the objects of a civil suit already pending in Superior Court).[31] This was the same Judge Joachimsen who had failed to issue a warrant for the arrest of the Bishop in 1890 but had issued a warrant for the arrest of Alexine and Ligda in the spring of 1891. (He had not tried their case, however; the Russian defendants had asked not to be tried by a Jewish judge because "there has been so much said and printed about the persecution of the Israelites by the Russians in the land of the Czar," and Joachimsen had granted the transfer). On this occasion, as on the previous one involving the Bishop, there is no indication that Joachimsen issued any warrant. The Bishop remained at large, though not for want of effort on the part of his enemies.

On September 19, a new meeting of Orthodox parishioners "of Greek, Russian, and Slavonian descent," eighty-strong according to Russel, took place. (The number of Russians among them, in any case, could not have much exceeded thirty, the newspaper's estimate of the total number of Russians in town.) Their resolutions, which were published in the papers the next day, re-endorsed the petition of June 1, 1889, and reiterated the complaints that made Vladimir "unworthy of the titles he bears and of the office he occupies." At the same meeting, another event transpired—one that did not make the newspapers: A committee of three (the Greek Cosma Constantin, the Montenegrin Gopchevich, and the Russian Zinger) was appointed to investigate the morals charges against the Bishop and to turn their findings over to the grand jury. Several days later the committee sent its petition, over Zinger's signature, to the foreman of the grand jury accompanied by documents "incriminating Vasilii Sokolovskii (known by the name of Bishop Vladimir) in unnatural crimes against morality committed in this city and state." These were the several written testimonies of the boys. The petition itself reviewed the history of the attempts to bring Vladimir to justice; declared that Horace Platt had bribed the mayor, Christopher A. Buckley, to use his influence to keep the case out of court; and added "several facts and rumors not mentioned in the documents. . . . "

Zinger called on the grand jury to remove from the Bishop's house the boy Korneliuk, the only remaining Russian victim of his crime, the others (the Martysh boys, Bobovsky, and Sanetskii [Vanna?]) having already been sent out of the country to Russia by the Bishop. He also called on the jury to get testimony from the boys Merkul'ev, Kochergin, and King, who had described their sexual relations with the Bishop in the appended letter to the monk, Father George, and were still living in the church.[32] Other persons from whom testimony should be collected included Levin's lawyer Myers, Russel, Platt, and two other individuals, all of whom had heard the boys' testimonies; the elder Martysh, now a priest in Alaska; and, finally, the captain of one of the Alaskan Trading Company ships who had allegedly surprised the Bishop engaged in sex with a boy named Eroshevich in the Bishop's cabin.[33]

Vladimir's opponents had put all their cards on the table.

According to Russel, word got out to the Bishop and the consulate about the documents being turned over to the grand jury, Vladimir realized the jig was finally up on the morals charges, and he got out of town. This may be so, but it seems more likely that that event was little more than a final encouragement to the Bishop to go along with the transfer process that had evidently begun as early as June and had become official with the Tsar's signature on the final order of transfer on September 7, but was not to be consummated until some time in November. It is not out of the question that the Bishop himself had initiated the transfer several months earlier; he said as much to the newspapers on October 4, when, in response to the appearance in the newspapers of a purported telegram from Petersburg announcing his transfer to a bishopric in Russia, he denied having received any official notice but admitted he had asked for a transfer "several months ago," "because his position here was so unpleasant he preferred to go back to Russia."[34]

This story may have been a little rear-guard action on the Bishop's part, but the fact remains that there is no sign a warrant was issued before he finally left town in November, no less than six weeks after Zinger turned over the materials to the grand jury, and Vladimir had been intrepid in the face of quite outrageous scandal up until then. Moreover, as late as October 23, consul Artsimovich, in an evident response to the September 19 petition by the anti-Vladimir parishioners, issued a circular "To the Greek Orthodox Parishioners of Alaska and the Aleutian Islands" denying still that the Bishop had been recalled and proclaiming his affairs in general to be in good order. After the signature of Artsimovich, as His Imperial Majesty's Consul-General in San Francisco, there followed those of eleven "officers and directors of the Greek Russian Slavonian Orthodox Eastern Church and Benevolent Society."[35]

But the Bishop had had enough and was, at last, on the way

out. In the second week of November, he, rather than Russel, "got quietly out of town." The last document in the consular records on Church affairs for these years is the indenture dated May 26, 1892, between Artsimovich and the new Bishop, Nicholas, conveying to Nicholas the Church's San Francisco properties that Artsimovich had been holding in trust since Vladimir's departure. It reveals that Vladimir had conveyed the property to Artsimovich on November 9. That was probably the last thing he did before leaving town.

The exact date of Russel's departure is not known, either. We know only that sometime in 1892 he and his wife left for Hawaii. Many years later, Russel explained their reason for leaving as the need "to rest from the fierce political and economic struggle of a large American city."[36] No doubt trying to keep up a medical practice and carry on the struggle against the Bishop at the same time required a good deal of energy, if that is what he was referring to, but Russel had enough time and energy left over to travel and write about California, and even to write, in 1890–91, a 900-page English-language manuscript on the Russian Orthodox Church, a by-product of his contest with the Bishop, which he entitled "The Levitical Caste in Russia."[37]

The fact that Russel was able to pursue such extensive literary projects at the very time his fight with Vladimir was reaching its height suggests that the controversy was damaging his practice: It split the small Orthodox community from which he apparently drew most of his clientele and, of course, raised questions about Russel's reputation as well as the Bishop's. Poor professional prospects may have caused the restless Russel to look afield once again now that victory of a sort had come in his contest with the Bishop. He never returned to California and San Francisco.

3

Later Adventures

Some of Dr. Russel's most-remarkable adventures lay still ahead. He continued his generally westward peregrinations, eventually settling in Japan and, ultimately, in China. Wherever he went he continued to practice medicine, to write about his new surroundings, and to stay involved in politics—always on the left.

Russel remained in the Hawaiian Islands, first on Oahu and then on Hawaii (with prolonged absences toward the end), until 1906. During these years, he practiced medicine most of the time, spent five years in an ultimately unsuccessful effort to

become a coffee planter, and got involved in Territorial politics after the 1898 annexation of Hawaii by the United States. Russel had opposed the sugar planters' Republic that had replaced the Kingdom in 1893 and took part in the formation of a Home Rule party to stand against the *haole*-dominated Republicans and Democrats in the elections to the first Territorial Legislature in November 1900. Russel emerged from these elections a senator, and in 1901 he became the first President of the Hawaiian Senate (he has been known ever since in the Russian literature as "Gavaiskii senator"—the Hawaiian Senator).

During the short tenure of the first Senate (1901–02), Russel feverishly drafted numerous more-or-less radical reform bills on such matters as land distribution, taxes, education, and alcohol control. (Russel was something of a specialist on alcoholism and a passionate proponent of abstinence; he believed that alcohol was a particular curse of the Russian people.) None of his bills became law: Those that made it—the alcohol bill not among them—through the legislature, where his Home Rule Party enjoyed only a plurality, were vetoed by the Republican governor, Sanford Dole.

Disenchanted with Territorial politics (he did not stand in the 1902 elections)[1] and with his coffee-plantation venture about to collapse, Russel moved on once again. His interest in the Russian revolutionary movement, and the fate of the political exiles in Siberia in particular, had been rekindled toward the end of his parliamentary episode by the unexpected arrival in Honolulu from Nagasaki of his old comrade from populist days, Lev Deutsch. Deutsch was en route to Europe from his escape eastward out of Siberian exile, following a fairly common trajectory in those days.[2] In October 1903, Russel sailed for Shanghai, by way of Japan, with a scheme for liberating Russian political prisoners from East-Siberian prisons near the Chinese border by means of an armed raid by Mongolian partisans across the frontier![3]

This, one of Russel's more fantastic schemes, was interrupted by the outbreak of the Russo-Japanese War in February 1904. In the spring of 1904, after spending a total of nine months in Shanghai, he returned to Hawaii. In a speech in the Honolulu Opera House and in several articles in the local paper, Russel excoriated the Russian imperialist Goliath and rooted for the Japanese David. As a result of this exposure, in the spring of 1905 he received an invitation from The Society of Friends of Russian Freedom in New York to go to Japan to help George Kennan conduct propaganda for political reform among Russian prisoners of war. Russel, who had met Kennan in San Francisco and had a high opinion of his efforts on behalf of Russian political prisoners, quickly agreed and set out for Japan in late May or early June of 1905. In Japan, Russel quickly took the direction of the political-enlightenment campaign into his hands, which included publishing a weekly Russian-language magazine, *Iaponiia i Rossiia* (Japan and Russia), distributing a lot of Russian-émigré literature sent from Europe by Kennan's and Russel's contacts, and giving lectures to the Russian internees. He kept this up until the Russian government, after the armistice had been signed in August 1905, managed to persuade the Japanese war ministry to put a stop to it.[4]

Unbeknownst to the liberal Kennan, Russel had a hidden revolutionary agenda, too. It was, if anything, even more fantastic than his Mongolian raid scheme. In a letter from Mountain View (Hawaiian Territories) to the Japanese consul general in Honolulu dated March 31, 1905 (that is, before he had been contacted by the Friends of Russian Freedom), Russel had on his own requested permission to agitate among Russian war prisoners in Japan for the purpose of forming from among them "the nucleus of the people's army." This force would be "transported and landed at some convenient point on Siberian shores" with ammunition and guns.[5] If we may believe Russel's much later account of the episode, his plan was "to cross 40,000 revolutionary prisoners over to Siberia in order to cut off [General] Linevich from his base and, together with the 30,000-strong Vladivostok garrison, to head for Moscow." Both the prisoners and the Japanese government were enthusiastic about the plan, he claimed, but it was vetoed by the Battle Organization of the Socialist Revolutionary Party in Petersburg (the heir to the populist terrorist organization of the late 1870s), with which he was in touch.[6]

Russel returned to Hawaii briefly in 1906 and there, apparently, was deprived of his U.S. passport and citizenship—ostensibly on grounds of his long absence from the country, but in fact, Russel claimed, because he had refused an order from the State Department, responding to protestations from the Russian ambassador in Washington, to desist from his agitational activity in Japan. Russel soon left Hawaii for the Far East, never to return.

Russel and his wife lived in Nagasaki until her death in 1910.[7] He then moved for a time to Mindanao in the Philippines, where he was reunited with his daughters from his first marriage, Vera and Maria. In 1915, during the First World War, he returned to Nagasaki and moved in with his two young sons, conceived during his earlier stay in Nagasaki, and their respective Japanese mothers, his former housemaids.

Russel naturally welcomed the February Revolution of 1917 that finally overthrew the Russian autocracy, but he did not join the wave of returning political exiles, apparently because of his age (he was now 66) and his complicated family situation. He opposed the seizure of power by the Bolsheviks in October because he believed it made Russia more vulnerable to German aggression; in this war, he supported Russia.[8] He supported the rebellion of the Czech legions against the Bolsheviks in the spring of 1918. As late as spring 1921, Russel told a Russian visitor that Bolshevism had grown out of the stupidity and ignorance of the Russian people, strengthened by its inveterate alcoholism. By the end of that year, however, Russel had changed his opinion

Russel with his grandsons in Japan

about the Bolsheviks, prompted by their abandonment of "war communism" and adoption of the relatively moderate New Economic Policy.

Russel left Japan in September 1920 and moved with his three Japanese children (a third had been born in 1919!) and one of his Japanese wives to the seaport of Tientsin, near Peking. In habitual fashion, he had apparently made himself unwelcome in Japan with his socialist opinions and his opposition to Japan's imperialist activities in Korea and China. In Tientsin, Russel opened a clinic in the British concession. In 1927, he became a member of the Soviet Association of Former Political Prisoners and began to receive a pension from it. Russel died in Tientsin on April 30, 1930. His ashes were returned to Japan in 1946 by one of his sons and were buried in the family tomb.[9]

4

Ho, to America!

Russel claimed that, as a revolutionary, he was interested only in the future, not the past. "It is time to cast off tradition and look at the world with our own eyes."[1] The fact is, of course, that Nicholas Russel came to the subject of life in America with a considerable baggage of Russian and generally European images and stereotypes about it. The opinions he expresses in "Around California" about Americans' obsession with money, their purely pragmatic turn of mind, and so on were common coin in the European tradition of writing about America.

The specifically Russian tradition of writing about America was already long and varied, going all the way back to the time of the American Revolution, which roughly coincided with—and could even be said to have inspired, in some measure—the birth of critical political and social thought in Russia. The prevailing stereotype of the Romantic age of the 1830s and 1840s—of America as a materialistic and soulless civilization ("It is a cold and calculating country," wrote Alexander Herzen) —was overlaid (but by no means obliterated) in the 1860s and 1870s, when Russel was coming of age, by the detailed, generally admiring, view of American life and institutions provided in the writings of people who had actually visited the country.[2]

As a member of the Russian populist generation of the 1870s, and an "Americanist" in his youth to boot, Russel came to America with ambivalent, even paradoxical, preconceptions: On the one hand, this was a great social experiment, the "land of the free," (as he described it in "Ho, to America!," a chapter in his autobiographical novel), where the individual personality could flourish and collectivist utopias could be established; on the other hand, America was the land of money-grubbing, of robber barons, monopolies, and the doctrine of "the devil take the hindmost." This ambivalence permeates his account of life in California.

In 1879, toward the end of his stay in Romania, Russel had drawn up a summary program of political and social change. It contained seven basic points:

1. Abolition of private ownership of the means of production, their transfer to collective ownership of the workers of field and factory. Guarantee to the worker of the totality of his production.

2. Suppression of competition and of the state of chaos in production, which leads to surpluses in world markets and causes economic crises.

3. Suppression of competition and hatred among nations, with all their consequences: wars, conquests, despotism, etc.

4. Political decentralization. Autonomy of communities. Creation of social organization from the bottom up; that is, on the basis of sympathies and reciprocal interests. Federalism.

5. Guarantee of equal general and professional education to all children. Guarantee of the instruments of labor, and thereby of the means of existence, to all adults of both sexes. Assistance in case of illness and old age. Balance of intellectual with physical labor so that the individual can develop harmoniously and universally.

6. Emancipation of the woman from the authority of the man.

7. Reorganization of the family on the exclusive basis of reciprocal sympathies and of economic, political, and social equality.

This program, Russel wrote, reflected the natural tendency of contemporary civilized society, which within a few decades (at most) would produce a social revolution.[3]

There is no reason to believe that Russel ever abandoned the general ideal embodied in this program. (His hostility toward the Bolsheviks in the early years of their regime was not over the principle of abolishing private ownership and the market.) Contrary to the claim of his somewhat younger fellow Russian-revolutionary immigrant to America—Peter Demens ("Tverskoi"), who became a successful entrepreneur in this country, author of many admiring works about America for Russian readers, and a Republican—Russel demonstrated that not every Russian radical becomes a Republican when transplanted to American soil.[4]

Russel takes a moment to enjoy his surroundings

Considering Russel's political-ideological background, his generally critical attitude toward American civilization is hardly surprising. He cannot conceal, however, his admiration for the Americans' ability to organize themselves spontaneously, their social self-discipline, and, above all, their capacity for practical inventiveness and problem solving—a characteristic he describes in the story (virtually an allegory) about the hydraulic water pipe, which the simple American miners invented but the St. Petersburg mining engineers on expense accounts were unable to copy. To be sure, Russel's love of nature, which is evident throughout his account, also led him to warn of the potentially disastrous ecological effects of unchecked American inventiveness.

Although Russel never returned to California after 1892, it seems his California interlude occupied a special place in his memory. "I dream of returning to my California," he wrote at age 76 to his Prague correspondent, "and somehow establishing myself there so as to be able to take up pen and paper. It is hard to forgo an active part in the struggle for a better future."[5]

Notes

Introduction

1. "They constituted themselves the arbiters of trade . . . They destroyed possible competitors . . . They exerted a terrorism over merchants and over communities . . . They participated in election contests . . . They menaced business, paralyzed capital, and retarded investment and development." *Report, Pacific Railway Commission*, p. 141; as quoted in Norman E. Tutorow, *Leland Stanford: Man of Many Careers* (Menlo Park, CA: Pacific Coast Publishers, 1971), p. 114. See also Oscar Lewis, *The Big Four: the Story of Huntington, Stanford, Hopkins, and Crocker, and of the Building of the Central Pacific* (New York: Knopf, 1938).

2. See Tutorow, *Leland Stanford*, p. 227, citing the *San Francisco Examiner*, June 22, 1893.

Part II

Chapter 1: *The Making of a Revolutionary in Exile*

1. Russel, N.J. (doctor in medicina), *Asupra methodei antiseptica de tratament in chirurgie* (Pitesci, 1877).

2. There are several biographies of Russel, including two books: Haruki Wada, *Nikolai Russel*, 2 vols. (Tokyo, 1973); and Mikhail Ivanovich Ios'ko, *Nikolai Sudzilovskii-Russel': zhizn', revoliutsionnaia deiatel'nost' i mirovozrenie* [life, revolutionary activity, and worldview]. The principal shorter treatments are I.I. Popov, "Nikolai Konstantinovich Russel-Sudzilovskii," *Katorga i ssylka* [Hard labor and exile], 1930, no. 6, pp. 168–176 (very unreliable), and S. Israel and J. Eskenazy, "Le révolutionnaire russe Nikolaj Constantinovič Sudzilovski-Russel en Roumanie et en Bulgarie," *Etudes Balkaniques* (Sofia), 1967, no. 7, pp. 163–190.

3. This tradition was well know in Russia. A description of Josiah Warren's anarchist settlement on Long Island, Modern Times, had appeared in the Russian press as early as 1865. A two-volume description of American utopian settlements published in 1867, William Hebworth Dixon's *New America* (London: Hurst & Blackett), was excerpted in the Russian press immediately upon its appearance, and a full-scale translation into Russian was published in Petersburg in the same year, 1867 (followed by another in 1869). See Robert V. Allen, *Russia Looks to America: the View to 1917* (Washington, D.C., 1988), pp. 37–38. Vladimir Debogorii's older cousin, Ivan Debogorii-Mokrievich, had visited America in 1868–69 and had spent some time in the Oneida Community. He may have been the first Russian to travel to the United States with the aim of establishing a communist settlement for Russian immigrants. See Avrahm Yarmolinsky, *A Russian's American Dream: a Memoir on William Frey* (Lawrence: The University of Kansas Press, 1965), pp. 12–13. The first American communes motivated by secular socialism dated to the 1820s. Yaacov Oved, *Two Hundred Years of American Communes* (New Brunswick: Transaction Books, 1988).

4. Russel tells this story in his lightly fictionalized autobiography (unpublished, in English), "One Man's Battle": TsGAOR [Central State Archive of the October Revolution, Moscow], coll. no. 5825, inventory 1, ch. V ("Ho, to America!").

5. Machtet spent some time in mid-1873 on a commune that had already been founded, in 1871, at Cedar Vale in southeastern Kansas by another Russian of similar intent and outlook, William Frey (Vladimir Konstantinovich Geins [Heinz], 1839–1888). Avrahm Yarmolinsky, *A Russian's American Dream: a Memoir on William Frey* (Lawrence: The University of Kansas Press, 1965).

6. See Olga Peters Hasty and Susanne Fusso, *America Through Russian Eyes, 1874–1926* (New Haven: Yale University Press, 1988), pp. 16–82.

7. The "Americans" were reproached: "You who have been nurtured physically and spiritually at the expense of the peasants' sweat and tears, are you going to abandon the people in their helplessness, slavery and ignorance? You are its eyes and mind. Your duty is to remain in Russia and put your life on the line for them in the struggle." Dr. Nikolai Russel, "V Ameriku" [To America], *Russkoe Slovo* (Russian-language newspaper), Tientsin, China, February 1, 1922.

8. Letter of N.K. Russel to A.N. Sletova (copy), dated Tientsin, December 29, 1928. TsGAOR, coll. 5825, item 171. See Ios'ko *Nikolai Sudzilovskii-Russel*, pp. 80–81, 153; and S. Israel and J. Eskenazy, "Le révolutionnaire russe," p. 167. Ios'ko claims that Russel was naturalized in 1892, but in the document he cites (incorrectly), Russel only states that this happened "during [his] stay in San Francisco" (p. 2). According to the Russian consular records (San Francisco), Russel applied to the Russian government for amnesty in 1889; he was notified of the rejection of his application in February, 1890. U.S. National Archives, Russian Consular Records (microfilm), San Francisco, box 64 (reel 143), nos. 360, 926.

9. His new wife, the widow Leokadiia Vikent'evna Regutenko (née Shebeko), had a medical degree from the University of Berne and had come to the Balkans as a military doctor attached to the Russian army in the Russo-Turkish war. She stayed on (at Ruse) to become, still according to the chroniclers, the first woman doctor in Bulgaria. Israel and Eskenazy, "Le révolutionnaire russe," p. 179.

10. In the course of these events, according to Evgenii L'vov (Kochetov), the correspondent in Bulgaria of the conservative Petersburg newspaper *Novoe vremia* (*New Times*), Russel, as the agent of the Bulgarian revolutionaries, made an attempt on his, L'vov-Kochetov's, life in the presence of the Russian consul in retaliation for L'vov-Kochetov's denunciations of their movement in his newspaper. "Happily for me," wrote L'vov-Kochetov, "the attempt was limited to a small wound in the back of the head and ended with the flight of Russel and his accomplices." Unfortunately, Russel's biographers fail to produce any corroborative evidence for L'vov-Kochetov's charges. E. L'vov (Russkii strannik), *Bolgariia v period terrora i anarkhii* [Bulgaria in time of terror and anarchy] (Moscow, 1888), p. v., as quoted in Israel and Eskenazy, "Le révolutionnaire russe," p. 180. Russel's Bulgarian biographers accept this story as fact. Ios'ko does not mention it.

11. TsGAOR, coll. 5825, item no. 10, leaf 93. In the early 1880s while in Paris, Russel, according to a confidante of the time, dreamed of "returning [sic] to

America to found there a mobile international clinic that could move from country to country." A. Vinitskaia [Aleksandra Budzianik], "Iz prikliuchenii v Parizhe (Pamiati P.L. Lavrov) [From my adventures in Paris (to the memory of P.L. Lavrov)], in *Istoricheskii vestnik*, 1912, no. 1, p. 134 (cited in Israel and Eskenazy, "Le révolutionnaire russe," p. 175, n. 79).

Chapter 2: *The Bishop and the Schoolboys*

1. Russian Consular Papers (San Francisco), box 64 (no pagination). Unlike his older brother and at least two older sisters, the much younger Emil (born ca. 1860?) seems to have been immune to the revolutionary urge. In San Francisco Emil was engaged in some kind of commerce. On May 18, 1888, he had written a letter to the Russian Emperor through the San Francisco consulate asking to be relieved of his status as a Russian subject in order to become a U.S. citizen and enjoy the full protection of American laws, which, he wrote, he needed in order to succeed in business. Eight months later, on January 21, 1889, he wrote to the consul-general, asking that this request be rescinded: His health couldn't tolerate "the American climate" and he wanted to be able to return to Russia. The Russian foreign ministry responded to both requests by informing the consulate that since he had overstayed the limit allowed on his passport, Emil would be held responsible for this breach of law when he returned to Russia. Emil's reaction to this news remains unknown to us.

2. This episode is somewhat mysterious. Why should Emil have called for the recall of the Bishop and then provided him with ammunition for the anathema against his own brother? Did the Bishop threaten him, too, with excommunication? Of course, the Bishop could simply have gotten some information about Russel's biography from Emil at some earlier time and called it "testimony" (*svidetel'stvo*). It is curious, however, that Russel makes no mention of his brother in his account of the Bishop Vladimir affair (except in reproducing the texts of the petition and the anathema), in his travelogue, or in any other accounts of his California sojourn seen by this writer. It is also curious that in the brochure on Russel put together some years later by his friend and fellow revolutionary fugitive, E.E. Lazarev, Emil's name is excised (twice) from an otherwise integrally reproduced text of the Bishop's anathema. Dr. N. Russel, *Zhitie Preosviashchennago Vladimira, byvshago episkopa Aleutskago i Aliaskinskago, nyne vikarnago episkopa Voronezhskago* [Life of the Right Reverend Vladimir, former Bishop of the Aleutians and Alaska, presently Suffragan Bishop of Voronezh] (Moscow:

pechatano v tipografii P. Pravdoliubova, 1895) (in fact, published abroad, perhaps in San Francisco). E.E. Lazarev, *Gavaiskii senator i vozhdi russkago pravoslaviia, Episkop Vladimir i K.P. Pobedonostsev* [The Hawaiian senator and the leaders of Russian Orthodoxy, Bishop Vladimir and K.P. Pobedonostsev] (Geneva: M. Elpidine, 1902).

3. Russel knew Pobedonostsev: back in 1868–69 Pobedonostsev had been his law professor at Petersburg University.

4. It also included the Russian far-eastern areas of Kamchatka and Okhotsk.

5. Russel, *Zhitie*, p. 10. Olarovskii to Pobedonostsev, April 2, 1886, Russian Consular Archives, box 64. Our only source on the rumors about Ioann is Russel. While he takes them at face value, it is unlikely that he made them up. According to Russel, Ioann had an illegitimate son by an American girl and was forced by the girl's mother to pay her $10,000—out of church funds, of course—for the child's upkeep. Apparently Pobedonostsev had Nikita defrocked after receiving Olarovskii's letter. (See Olarovskii's letter to K.V. Struve, Russian Ambassador in Washington, May 14, 1886, Russian Consular Archives, box 64.

6. One Kovrygin, who, among other things, according to the *San Francisco Examiner*, denounced Kedrolivanskii to the Church authorities in St. Petersburg for separating from his wife (Kedrolivanskii belonged to the "white," or non-celibate, clergy; bishops had to be of the "black," or celibate, clergy).

7. *San Francisco Chronicle*, June 11, 1988. Russel, *Zhitie*, pp. 12–15, 21.

8. *San Francisco Examiner*, May 23, 1889.

9. Russel, *Zhitie*, pp. 19–21. In their seventh point the petitioners showed that they subscribed to the theory that the church had burned down through neglect brought on by the firing of the caretaker.

10. Russel, *Zhitie*, pp. 22–23. Vladimir also accused Russel of "wearing the mask of a Christian in order to have a greater chance of sending the Bishop to a monastery." The Bishop was probably at least half-right about this: Russel certainly did not observe Orthodox ritual, and he probably was not a Christian in any formal sense of the word except for having been baptized. He probably joined the Benevolent Society for social and professional reasons.

11. Russel, *Zhitie*, pp. 23–25. We have only Russel's account of the Martysh case. In cases involving the Bishop's relations with several other boys there is outside evidence, including handwritten autograph testimony by the boys themselves. These were scrupulously preserved by Russel and can be found in his archive (TsGAOR, coll. 5825, folder 15).

12. Russel, *Zhitie*, pp. 25–30, 39–42.

13. By November 1889, the consulate was getting telegraph inquiries from the foreign ministry and Pobedonostsev: "Is Bobovsky Bishop affair true?—Olarovskii." "What is about [sic] new scandal Wladimir Russel ask information—Pobedonostzoff." The San Francisco newspapers, however, despite their obvious appetite for sensation surrounding the Russian Church, studiously skirted the subject to the end, going no further than noting that questions were being raised about Vladimir's moral character. At the height of the scandal, one paper titillated its readers with the report that the Bishop was being accused of "crimes so repugnant that they could not even be hinted of in a public print"; but that was as far is it went, perhaps out of fear of libel suits or in conformity with some canon of propriety.

14. "Would any discredit or disgraceful fact be brought out against them?" Niebaum to Platt, January 13, No. 7. Russian Consular Records, box 64.

15. Platt to Niebaum, January 20, 1890. Russian Consular Records, box 64. According to the September 1891 petition of the anti-Vladimir group to the grand jury, Platt had himself interviewed several of the boys and taken their testimony in his office in January 1890. (See below).

16. Russel, *Zhitie*, pp. 33–35.

17. This act of the Bishop made it unlikely, Acting Consul Niebaum reported to his superior in Petersburg on February 11, that Russel could be brought to any kind of settlement out of court. He also let it be known that he considered the Bishop to be guilty of the charges. Niebaum to Aleksander Egorovich [Olarovskii?], February 11, 1890 (copy). Russian Consular Records, box 64.

18. *San Francisco Examiner*, August 29, 1891. The telegram was carefully preserved by Russel. TsGAOR, coll. 5825, folder 15, p. 30. "Process" means "trial."

Around California in 1891

19. *San Francisco Examiner,* August 29, 1891; Russel's Russian version curiously bears another signature: "Vlangali." Russel, *Zhitie,* p. 20.

20. Russel, *Zhitie,* pp. 36–37. Russel claimed that he, too, had received confidential letters from Pobedonostsev describing Vladimir as a mental case, which he had returned to their author at the latter's request. It is less than obvious how Russel could have come by these documents; it is possible they were provided by acting consul Niebaum, who was ill disposed toward Vladimir, thought he was guilty, and wanted him removed. Vladimir, in any event, himself confirmed to the newspapers that Inokentii was in the area at this time and had been charged to look into the situation of the Church. He also confirmed, in February 1890, that he had been summoned to Petersburg, but not recalled—only to give an accounting of the charges against him; he would probably leave in about three weeks; it would take that long for Inokentii, "who has been ordered from Petersburg to take charge during my absence," to get to San Francisco.

21. *San Francisco Chronicle,* August 28, 1891: "Bishop Vladimir: His Bitter Talk Against His Enemies."

22. Russian Consular Records, box 64: Report to Russian Mission in Washington, date March 11, 1890 (copy); Communication from Bishop Vladimir to consulate, February 29, 1890 (no. 36); Report to Washington, no. 187 (copy).

23. In April 1888, Platt had written a letter to the Russian consul-general, A.E. Olarovskii, explaining how Olarovskii, as administrator of a drowned predecessor's estate, could execute a deed of the Greek Church property to the new Bishop, Vladimir. In May 1892, an indenture was drawn up between the new consul-general, V.A. Artsimovich, and Vladimir's successor, Bishop Nicholas. Artsimovich had been holding the property in trust since Vladimir's departure in November 1891. These instruments are in the consular records.

24. The previous history of the case was recounted in a petition to the grand jury submitted by the anti-Vladimir group of parishioners in September 1891. Russel, *Zhitie,* p. 40.

25. Russian Consular Records, box 64, following letter of Russel to the consul-general (Niebaum), dated January 2, 1891.

26. Russian Consular Records, box 64: Russel to Vladimir (copy in Russel's hand), dated January 2, 1891. Russel did not use the high-fallutin' latin words "sodomist" and "castrate;" he employed much more graphic, colloquial Slavic expressions.

27. Russian Consular Records, box 64: Russel to Niebaum, January 2, 1891; Niebaum to Russel (copy), dated January 7; Niebaum to Struve (copy), dated January 8. Gustav Niebaum was an American citizen (born in Finland of Russian-German origin, naturalized) and a businessman (Alaska Fur Seal Company). He was also a Lutheran, which may be the key to Vladimir's hostility toward the consulate during Niebaum's stewardship.

28. *San Francisco Examiner,* May 16, 17. More or less simultaneously, Levin's younger brother, Boris, filed a suit against the Bishop to collect two years' wages ($1,100). Russian Consular Records, box 64: Platt to Niebaum, May 25, 1891.

29. The three of them, co-signed a letter to Father George of the Russian Church, dated December 31, 1890, describing in fairly graphic terms their alleged sexual relations with the Bishop. This letter became part of Russel's collection. TsGAOR, coll. 5825, folder 15, p. 31.

30. TsGAOR, coll. 5825, folder 15, pp. 40, 41, 42.

31. TsGAOR, coll. 5825, folder 15, p. 36.

32. These were the apparently half-breed boys who were among those removed from the seminary in the May raid.

33. Russel, *Zhitie*, pp. 39–42.

34. *San Francisco Examiner,* October 4, 1891.

35. Russian Consular Records, box 64. E.P. Alexine signed as treasurer. The *Chronicle* for October 24 carried a story on this circular. Russel's *Zhitie* for some reason misdates the Artsimovich circular to July 1890 (p. 37).

36. TsGAOR, coll. 5825, folder 171, p. 1.

37. TsGAOR, coll. 5825, folder 15. I haven't seen this manuscript. Judging from the title, Russel probably developed in this work the view of the Orthodox clergy that he outlines in the introduction to his "Life of Vladimir": a poorly educated, venal, unrespected, and morally bankrupt hereditary caste.

Chapter 3: *Later Adventures*

1. "The democratic comedy provoked a physiological revulsion in me," he later wrote to A.N. Sletova, recalling those days. TsGAOR, coll. 5825, folder 171, p. 4. On Russel's adventures in Hawaiian politics, see Ronald Hayashida and David Kittelson, "The Odyssey of Nicholas Russel," *The Hawaiian Journal of History* 11 (1977), pp. 110–124.

2. Leo Deutsch, *Sixteen Years in Siberia* (London, 1903).

3. N.K. Sudzilovskii (Russel), "Posleslovie" [afterword] to the Russian translation of George Kennan's article on propaganda amongst Russian prisoners of war in Japan in 1905, *Katorga i ssylka* [Forced labor and exile] 1927:2 (31), pp. 165–176.

4. George Kennan, "How Russian Soldiers were Enlightened in Japan," *Outlook*, March 17, 1915. On George Kennan, author of *Siberia and the Exile System*, see Frederick F. Travis, *George Kennan and the American-Russian Relationship* 1865–1924 (Athens, Ohio: Ohio University Press, 1990).

5. I wish to thank Eiko Kuwana for helping me to obtain a copy of this letter from the Diplomatic Record Office, Ministry of Foreign Affairs of Japan. Russel kept a copy of the same letter in his personal archive: TsGAOR, coll. 5825, folder 216.

6. TsGAOR, coll. 5825, folder 110. Russel to V. Gurevich, Director of the Prague Russian Archive, September 17, 1926. Russel attributed the Battle Organization's veto of his plan to Azef, its head, who was later revealed to be a police agent. General N.P. Linevich was the commander of Russian armies in the Far East. Russel had heard that the Vladivostok garrison was in revolt.

7. Hayashida and Kittelson write that the Russels separated at this point, with Mrs. Russel remaining in Hawaii. There is good evidence, however, that she went

with her husband to Nagasaki, where she died on January 3, 1910. See Ios'ko, *Nikolai Sudzilovskii-Russel*, p. 260. Russel's Japanese biographer, Wada, confirms this.

8. Russel believed, in fact, that the Russian autocracy was a Germanic or Prussian bureaucratic implant. (This was a fairly widespread idea among the Russian intelligentsia, dating back to the 1840s). Russel had hotly rejected George Kennan's suggestion in 1915, before America entered the war, that a replay of the 1905 political-enlightenment project might be carried on among Russian prisoners of war in Germany: "We are revolutionists in Russia *because* of the German yoke, because we have long ago found out that the predatory eagle's head and body are in Berlin, his right wing in Vienna, and the left in St. Petersburg." The thing to do was enlighten *German* prisoners of war in Russia, France, and England. TsGAOR, coll. 5825, folder 50: "To Russian political exiles and 'The American Friends of Russian Freedom'." (1915).

9. This information about Russel's last years comes, with the help of Eiko Kuwana, from Volume Two of Haruki Wada's Japanese biography of Russel.

Chapter 4: *Ho, to America!*

1. TsGAOR, coll. 5825, folder 110. Russel to Gurevich, September 17, 1926. "There is the past and there is the future. Only the latter is interesting."

2. See Hans Rogger, "America in the Russian Mind—or Russian Discoveries of America," *Pacific Historical Review*, 1978, no. 1, pp. 27–51. Herzen's generation drew its images of America from such sources as Tocqueville's *Democracy in America* (1835 and 1840). Russel's was exposed to sympathetic Russian accounts, such as P.I. Ogorodnikov's *Ot N'iu Iorka do San Frantsisko i obratno v Rossiiu* [From New York to San Francisco and back to Russia] (1872) (a second edition was titled *V strane svobody* [In the land of liberty] [1882]). Ogorodnikov, as Rogger points out, was aware of American defects, such as corruption in politics and the preoccupation with the pursuit of wealth, but considered venality the tribute paid by Americans for real self-government and materialism the condition of individual liberty and well-being.

3. Israel and Eskenazy, "Le révolutionnaire russe," p. 173. The program dates to 1879.

4. On Demens (the name he took in America), see Hans Rogger, "America Enters the Twentieth Century: the View from Russia," Inge Auerbach, Andreas Hillgruber, and Gottfried Schramm, eds., *Felder und Vorfelder russischer Geschichte: Studien zu Ehren von Peter Scheibert* (Freiburg, 1985), pp. 160–177; and Allen, *Russia Looks to America*, pp. 152–153 et passim.

5. TsGAOR, coll. 5825, folder 110. Russel to Gurevich, September 17, 1926.

About the Author

Terence Emmons is married and has two children. He enjoys long walks and is a Sunday carpenter, neither of which pastimes is unusual for one who was born and grew up in Salem, Oregon.

Prof. Emmons completed his undergraduate schooling at the University of Washington, received his PhD from the University of California at Berkeley in 1965, and has taught at Stanford ever since. A specialist in Russian history, he also teaches an honors course on historical method. He has visited the Soviet Union frequently since spending the years 1962–64 at Moscow University as a graduate student.

Prof. Emmons is co-director of an American-Soviet project for the compilation of a definitive bibliography of Russian émigré memoirs. He has written numerous scholarly articles and three books relating to Russian history, most recently *Time of Troubles: the Diary of Yurii Vladimirovich Got'e,* published by the Princeton University Press in 1988. Between 1974 and 1983 he was editor and publisher of *The Russian Review,* America's only scholarly journal devoted entirely to Russian affairs.

The Portable Stanford Book Series is grateful to the librarians at the Bancroft Library and California State Library, to Beverly Cola of The El Dorado County Historical Museum, and to Lolita Mattei, all of whom contributed greatly to the selection of photographs for this book.

The Portable Stanford Book Series

This is a volume of the Portable Stanford Book Series, published by the Stanford Alumni Association. Subscribers receive each new Portable Stanford volume on approval. The following books may also be ordered, by number, on the adjoining card:

$12.95 titles

- *Around California in 1891* by Terence Emmons (#4060)
- *Technology and Culture: A Historical Romance* by Barry M. Katz (#4057)
- *2020 Visions: Long View of a Changing World* by Richard Carlson and Bruce Goldman (#4055)
- *"What Is to Be Done?" Soviets at the Edge* by John G. Gurley (#4056)
- *Brief Lessons in High Technology: Understanding the End of This Century to Capitalize on the Next* edited by James Meindl (#4045)
- *Terra Non Firma: Understanding and Preparing for Earthquakes* by James M. Gere and Haresh C. Shah (#4030)

$10.95 titles

- *Notable or Notorious? A Gallery of Parisians* by Gordon Wright (#4052)
- *This Boy's Life* by Tobias Wolff (#4050)
- *Ride the Tiger to the Mountain: T'ai Chi for Health* by Martin and Emily Lee and JoAn Johnstone (#4047)
- *Alpha and Omega: Ethics at the Frontiers of Life and Death* by Ernlé W.D. Young (#4046)
- *Conceptual Blockbusting* (3rd edition) by James L. Adams (#4007)
- *In My Father's House: Tales of an Unconformable Man* by Nancy Huddleston Packer (#4040)
- *The Imperfect Art: Reflections on Jazz and Modern Culture* by Ted Gioia (#4048)
- *Yangtze: Nature, History, and the River* by Lyman P. Van Slyke (#4043)
- *The Eagle and the Rising Sun: America and Japan in the Twentieth Century* by John K. Emmerson and Harrison M. Holland (#4044)
- *The Care and Feeding of Ideas* by James L. Adams (#4042)
- *The American Way of Life Need Not Be Hazardous to Your Health* (Revised Edition) by John W. Farquhar, M.D. (#4018)
- *Cory Aquino and the People of the Philippines* by Claude A. Buss (#4041)
- *Under the Gun: Nuclear Weapons and the Superpowers* by Coit D. Blacker (#4039)
- *50: Midlife in Perspective* by Herant Katchadourian, M.D. (#4038)

- *Wide Awake at 3:00 A.M.: By Choice or By Chance?* by Richard M. Coleman (#4036)
- *Hormones: The Messengers of Life* by Lawrence Crapo, M.D. (#4035)
- *Panic: Facing Fears, Phobias, and Anxiety* by Stewart Agras, M.D. (#4034)
- *Who Controls Our Schools? American Values in Conflict* by Michael W. Kirst (#4033)
- *Matters of Life and Death: Risks vs. Benefits of Medical Care* by Eugene D. Robin, M.D. (#4032)
- *On Nineteen Eighty-Four* edited by Peter Stansky (#4031)
- *The Musical Experience: Sound, Movement, and Arrival* by Leonard G. Ratner (#4029)
- *Challenges to Communism* by John G. Gurley (#4028)
- *Cosmic Horizons: Understanding the Universe* by Robert V. Wagoner and Donald W. Goldsmith (#4027)
- *Beyond the Turning Point: The U.S. Economy in the 1980s* by Ezra Solomon (#4026)
- *The Age of Television* by Martin Esslin (#4025)
- *Insiders and Outliers: A Procession of Frenchmen* by Gordon Wright (#4024)
- *Mirror and Mirage: Fiction by Nineteen* by Albert J. Guerard (#4023)
- *The Touch of Time: Myth, Memory, and the Self* by Albert J. Guerard (#4022)
- *The Politics of Contraception* by Carl Djerassi (#4020)
- *Economic Policy Beyond the Headlines* by George P. Shultz and Kenneth W. Dam (#4017)
- *Tales of an Old Ocean* by Tjeerd van Andel (#4016)
- *Law Without Lawyers: A Comparative View of Law in China and the United States* by Victor H. Li (#4015)
- *The World That Could Be* by Robert C. North (#4014)
- *America: The View from Europe* by J. Martin Evans (#4013)
- *An Incomplete Guide to the Future* by Willis W. Harman (#4012)
- *Murder and Madness* by Donald T. Lunde, M.D. (#4010)
- *The Anxious Economy* by Ezra Solomon (#4009)
- *The Galactic Club: Intelligent Life in Outer Space* by Ronald Bracewell (#4008)
- *Is Man Incomprehensible to Man?* by Philip H. Rhinelander (#4005)
- *Some Must Watch While Some Must Sleep* by William E. Dement, M.D. (#4003)
- *Human Sexuality: Sense and Nonsense* by Herant Katchadourian, M.D. (#4002)